Henry B. Grant

Drill Tactics for Knights of Honor

Henry B. Grant

Drill Tactics for Knights of Honor

ISBN/EAN: 9783743317567

Manufactured in Europe, USA, Canada, Australia, Japa

Cover: Foto ©ninafisch / pixelio.de

Manufactured and distributed by brebook publishing software (www.brebook.com)

Henry B. Grant

Drill Tactics for Knights of Honor

DRILL TACTICS

FOR

KNIGHTS OF HONOR

SWORD AND BUGLE SIGNALS; RULES FOR COMPETITIVE DRILLS; MILITARY ORDERS AND CORRESPONDENCE; CEREMONIES AND HINTS FOR KNIGHTLY COURTESIES, ETC., ETC.

PUBLISHED BY AUTHORITY OF THE SUPREME LODGE KNIGHTS OF HONOR

By H. B. GRANT,

(Late) Captain U. S. A.

CINCINNATI:

THE PETTIBONE M'F'G CO.,

FRATERNITY PUBLISHERS.

1888.

Entered according to an Act of Congress, in the year 1888, by The Pettibone Mfg. Co., in the office of the Librarian of Congress, at Washington, D. C.

Contents.

Preface.	5
Definitions.	7
School of the Knight	10
Manual of the Sword	28
Silent Manual	42
Salutes	14, 43
School of the Officer	45
School of the Commandery	49
The Display Drill	86
School of the Battalion	160
Dress Parade	195
Review	200
General Parade	204
Sword Signals	256
Bugle Signals—33 Signals, 1 March.	208
Award of Prize and Rules for Competitive Drill	216
Index	219

Preface.

The favor with which the military works of the author have been received is a source of gratification to him and his publishers, while the fact that his original and assimilated movements, ceremonies and engravings have been copied by other authors, may, without vanity, be accepted as an evidence of the sincerity of the flattering approval bestowed upon them.

This system of Drill enjoys the commendation of educated tacticians and the official endorsement of five different semi military orders. It is again launched as a candidate for further recognition.

These Orders seem to be alive to the truth that respect for themselves and their orders demand that their drills should not only be based upon the tactics of the country, but that the commands and movements should be cl sely assimilated thereto. The formations are under separate "schools," and in harmony with the basis established by educated experience. Commanderies can therefore practice the "leg timate drill" alone or indulge in the display movements *ad libitum*. The assimilated display drills are clearly defined and separated in this work, the object being to make explanations so full that every one may know exactly what to do and how to do it.

The author does not claim any great amount of originality, although his work has been copied by the page, with slight modifications; and some of the cuts have been taken entire by other authors.

He trusts his efforts will meet with the approval of his brethren.

Definitions of Military Terms.

ABOUT. A wheel (or face) of 180°. *Full About:* a wheel of 360°.

BATTALION. Two or more commanderies, as prescribed.

CADENCE. The rate of regular planting of the feet in marching or succession of motions in the manual.

CAUTION. A direction to men under arms; or command given in an undertone, to indicate a contemplated movement or to correct an error.

COLUMN. A number of subdivisions formed in lines one behind the other.

COLUMN OF FILES. A single or double rank faced to the right or left (into column).

COMMANDERY DISTANCE. A distance equal to the front of the commandery when in line.

COUNTERMARCH. A change of direction to the rear; equivalent to "Column right (or left) march," executed twice in immediate succession.

COVER. Files or guides cover when exactly behind or in rear of each other, marching or at a halt

DEPLOY. To extend; a column "extended" into line.

DISTANCE. Space between Knights or subdivisions, measured in depth (perpendicular to the front).

DIVISION. One-half (one-third or one-fourth) more or less of the commandery. (In the army drill called *Platoon*.)

DOUBLE-SECTION. Twelve Knights in line, single or double rank. If double rank the front is the same (12).

DRILL CORPS. A portion of the commandery, with a head and members, organized for drilling.

ECHELON. Subdivisions in lines at equal distances, like stair steps, one more advanced than the other.

FACING DISTANCE is such that in facing to the right or left, into line, the elbows will touch.

FILE. A Knight in rank. Two or more Knights, one behind the other.

FILE LEADER. The Knight in front of the file whom the others of the file *cover or follow*.

FLANK. Either extremity of a line or side of a column.

INTERVAL. Space between Knights or subdivisions in line, measured parallel to the front.

LINE. Knights formed abreast, that is, elbow to elbow.

MARCHING FLANK. The extremity of the line farthest from the pivot, in the wheelings

MOTION. A distinct movement in the manual of the sword, without pause, and designated as *first motion*, *second motion*, etc.

PIVOT. The Knight on the flank upon whom the wheeling is made.

POST. Position or place prescribed.

RANK. A number of Knights in line.

RIGHT IN FRONT is when the original right of the line is the head of the column. The reverse is *left in front*.

Roster. List of officers and Knights for duty

Schedule. A programme containing the movements, etc., to be executed.

Section. Six Knights in line, single or double rank. If double rank, the front is the same (6).

Squad. A small detachment of Knights. It may be (in mounted drill is) used in preparatory, in l.eu of "Knights."

Squadron. Two commanderies mounted; in this work two commanderies of a battalion, as prescribed.

Subdivision. Threes, sections, etc. A commandery sub divided.

Wheel. A circular movement by which a line of two or more Knights is placed at right angles to its former position.

Wheeling Distance is such that in wheeling into line the subdivisions will exactly join those on the right and left; or the distance between subdivisions equal to the front of the subdivision.

Wing. One-half of a line. One of the Grand Divisions into which a line may be divided.

School of the Knight.

INTRODUCTION.

The instruction of Knights in the drill can only be perfected by joining theory to practice.

A competent officer should be detailed to drill a squad in the School of the Knight before the men are permitted to drill with the commandery. Stated times for drill, faithfully improved, are essential to success. A well disciplined commandery will rarely be troubled about "a constitutional number" at its conclaves.

In this work commands are given for the execution of movements toward both right and left flanks, but the explanation of the movement toward one flank only will be made. To obtain the explanation toward the other flank substitute *left* for *right*, or the reverse.

The last syllable of a command determines its prompt execution.

When commands are prescribed herein, without mention as to who should give them, it will be understood that they are given by the officer in charge.

The movements and commands in the School of the Knight apply with equal force in other parts of this work wherever instruction to the contrary is not given, substituting *commandery, detachment, double-section* or *division*, etc , for *Knights* or *Squad*.

COMMANDS.

Commands should be given in a clear, animated tone, every syllable distinct and loud enough to be heard without difficulty by every Knight under instruction. If the lines are subdivided, the commands may be briskly repeated by the officers in charge of subdivisions, if necessary, in a lower tone, but loud enough to be heard by their particular section or division. The failure of a single Knight to understand the command may throw the entire line into confusion.

Commands are of two kinds:

1. *Preparatory*, such as *forward, carry*, etc., [printed in *italics*] indicates the movement to be executed.
2. Of *execution*, such as MARCH, SWORDS, etc. [printed in SMALL CAPITALS], pronounced in a firm, brief tone, indicates the exact instant for commencing, and causes the execution of a movement.

A preparatory command should always precede and be understood before adding that of execution. The cadence of commands is determined by the step.

This is the general rule, which does not rigidly apply to the double time. Regularity in the cadence of commands should be habitual, but undue delay after the preparatory command is given is irritating and demoralizing.

POSITION.

Heels on the same line, as near each other as the formation of the Knight will permit. If one heel be in rear of the other, one shoulder will be thrown back and the position is constrained. Men knock kneed, or with large calves, can not, without constraint, make their heels touch while standing.

The *feet* turned out equally, forming with each other an angle of about sixty degrees. If one is turned out more than the other the shoulders will be deranged; if both are turned out too much, the upper part of the body can not be inclined forward without making the position unsteady.

The *knees* straight without stiffness. If stiffened constraint and fatigue will be unavoidable.

The *body* erect upon the hips, inclining a little forward. This gives equilibrium to the position The reverse is common—that is, throwing the shoulders back and projecting the belly, which causes inconvenience in marching and fatigue.

The *shoulders* square and falling equally. Many have a bad habit of dropping one shoulder. Correct it at once.

The *arms* hanging naturally;

The *elbows* near the body;

The *palms* of the *hands* turned slightly to the front, hands open, fingers together and nearly straight the little fingers behind the seams of the pantaloons. These prevent Knights from occupying unnecessary space in ranks and tend to keep the shoulders in.

The *head* erect and square to the front;

The *chin* slightly drawn in, without constraint Stiffness in these positions wi'l be communicated to other parts of the body, giving pain and fatigue.

The *eyes* straight to the front, striking the ground at about the distance of fifteen yards The surest way to keep the shoulders in line and head erect. Insist upon it.

When the Knights appreciate the importance and understand the details of the position—the *alpha* of the tactics—pass to the next lesson.

SCHOOL OF THE KNIGHT.

Let the Knights rest often for a few minutes at a time, until they become easy in their *position;* for this purpose command

REST.

All are now at liberty to stand, sit, or lie down, but not to move more than two or three yards away, nor is silence required.

Wishing to relieve the attention merely, command

1. *In place.* 2. REST.

The immobility or silence need not then be preserved, but the left heel ought to be kept in its place.

1. *Knights.* 2 ATTENTION.

At the first command quiet is restored; and at the second every Knight promptly takes his position, remains motionless and fixes his attention.

1. *Break ranks.* 2. MARCH.

This dismisses the squad.

1. *Eyes.* 2. RIGHT (or LEFT). 3. FRONT.

At the command *right*, each Knight will turn his head promptly but gently, so as to bring the inner corner of the left eye on a line with the center of the body, the eyes fixed on the eyes of the Knights in, or supposed to be in, the same rank (This is the position of head and eyes in *right dress*, except that the Knight on the extreme right does not turn the head, but remains at *attention*) Retain this position until the command *front* is given, when the head and eyes resume the habitual position.

Eyes left is exactly the reverse of *eyes right.*

See that every motion is understood and properly executed before passing to the next; but do not dwell too long upon any one, lest a dislike be engendered for the work at the beginning. Be clear and plain in every explanation, cause each Knight by himself to execute the motions, and correct any defect as soon as discovered. While courtesy is extended to all, *the discipline in ranks should be impartially rigid*.

SALUTES WITH THE HAND.

1. *Right* (or *left*) *hand*. 2. SALUTE.

First motion: Raise the right hand till the tips of the fingers touch the visor opposite the right eye, thumb closed, fingers and hand extended in prolongation of the fore arm, elbow down. *Second motion:* Lower the hand briskly to the right until the points of the fingers are at the height of the shoulder and in front of it, elbow advanced, hand and fingers still extended in prolongation of the fore arm. *Third motion:* Drop the hand to the side.

When in uniform the proper salute should not be omitted, but the etiquette of Knightly Courtesy strictly observed. This should be impressed upon the minds as other lessons are taught, by theory and practice.

A junior officer or Knight, addressing a senior, salutes first, which is always acknowledged. If the senior officer addresses a junior officer or Knight the inferior in rank makes the first salute

If the sword is in the scabbard the salute is with the hand.

1. *Right* (or *left*) 2. FACE.

At the command *face*, raise the right foot slightly, face to the right, turning on the left heel the left toe slightly raised; replace the right heel by the side of the left and on the same line.

The facings to the left are executed on the same heel as the facings to the right.

1. *Knights.* 2. About. 3. Face.

At the command *about*, turn on the left heel, bring the left toe to the front, carry the right foot to the rear, the hollow opposite to and three inches from the left heel, the feet square to each other. At the command *face*, raise the toes a little, turn on both heels, and face to the rear. When the face is nearly completed, raise the right foot and replace it by the side of the left.

1. Parade. 2 Rest.

This gives rest, imposing both steadiness and attention.

At the command *rest*, carry the right foot three inches directly to the rear, the left knee slightly bent; clasp the hands in front of the center of the body, the left hand uppermost, the left thumb clasped by the thumb and forefinger of the right hand.

1. *Knights* 2. Attention.

Resume the position of a Knight in line.

THE STEPS.

The length of the direct step in *common* and *quick time* is thirty inches, measured from heel to heel.

The cadence for *common time* is ninety steps per minute; for *quick time,* one hundred and twenty steps per minute.

The length of the *double step* is thirty-five inches; the cadence is one hundred and eighty steps per minute.

The *side step* is six inches.

The *backward step* and *short step* are each fifteen inches, measured from heel to heel.

All steps are executed in quick time unless otherwise specified.

A natural swinging of the left hand, describing twelve inches of an inverted arc of a circle, is proper.

1. *Balance step.* 2. *Left* (or *right*) *foot.* 3. Forward.
4. Rear. 5 Halt.

The principles of the direct step are taught thus:

Require the body, shoulders, arms and hands of the Knights to be kept in *position.* (See page 11.)

At the command *forward,* bend the left knee slightly and carry the left foot, without jerk, about fourteen inches to the front, straightening the knee as the foot is brought forward, the toe turned out and slightly depressed, the sole of the foot about three inches from the ground, the body balanced firmly on the right foot and inclined slightly forward.

At the command *rear,* carry the left foot, without jerk, to the rear, the knee slightly bent, the toe on a line with the heel and inclining slightly downward.

At the command *halt,* plant the foot by the side of the other. Now exercise with the other foot.

1. *Balance step.* 2. *Left foot.* 3. Forward. 4. Ground.
5 Halt.

At *forward,* advance the left foot as before.

At the command *ground,* plant it without shock, the foot advancing as the weight of the body is brought forward, the left heel thirty inches from the right; the right foot is then advanced to the position of *forward* without command, and similarly planted at the command *ground.*

At the command *halt* the foot in advance is planted, and the one in rear brought to its side.

Commence at a very slow cadence, afterward increase it to *common time.* When this is well understood, command

1. *Forward.* 2. *Common time.* 3. March.

At the command *forward* throw the weight of the body upon the right leg, without bending the knees.

SCHOOL OF THE KNIGHT. 17

At the command *march* move the left foot smartly, but without jerk, thirty inches straight forward, observing carefully the principles explained in the *balance steps;* do not cross the legs or strike one against the other; eyes to the front.

Indicate the cadence by counting *one, two.* Do *not* call out "*hep, hep,*" but instruct the squad that the left foot is planted the instant the odd number is called.

1. *Knights,* 2. HALT.

At the command *halt*, given when either foot is being brought to the ground, plant the foot and bring the foot in rear to its side and plant it without shock.

1. *Forward.* 2. MARCH,

Is the command to march in *quick time* from a halt, always stepping off with the left foot first.

The change to any other cadence is indicated by naming the time before the command *march*, thus: 1. *Common time.* 2. MARCH; or 1. *Double time.* 2. MARCH; or if at a halt, the same commands preceded by *forward*, thus: 1. *Forward.* 2. *Common time.* 3. MARCH, stepping off with the left foot as before.

1. *Short step.* 2. MARCH.

Being in march, at the second command the length of the step is reduced to fifteen inches without changing the cadence; at the command, 1. *Forward.* 2. MARCH, the full step is resumed.

1. *Mark time.* 2. MARCH.

Being in march, the second command, given when either foot is coming to the ground, continue the cadence and make a semblance of marching, without gaining ground, by alternately advancing each foot about half its length, the sole parallel with the ground, and bringing it back on a line with the other.

To resume the direct step the command is: 1. *Forward.* 2. March.

1. *Change step.* 2. MARCH.

At the second command, given the instant either foot strikes the ground, the other foot is advanced and planted; bring the hollow of the foot that is in rear against the heel of the foot in front, and step off promptly with the foot that is in front, carefully keeping up the cadence.

1. *Backward.* 2. MARCH.

Step off with the left foot fifteen inches straight to the rear, measured from heel to heel. At the command, 1. *Knights*, 2. HALT, plant the foot that is in rear and bring the other to its side.

1. *To the rear.* 2. MARCH.

Being in march; at the second command, given as the right foot strikes the ground, advance the left foot to the full step distance and plant it; face to the rear turning to the right on the balls of both feet, and immediately step off with the left foot.

1. *Right* (or *left*) *side-step.* 2. MARCH.

At the second command carry the right foot six inches to the right, keeping the knees straight, shoulders square to the front, heels on the same line; plant the righ' foot and bring the left to its side and so continue, observing the cadence, until halted.

SCHOOL OF THE KNIGHT.

1. *Double step.* 2. MARCH.

At the first command raise the hands, fingers closed, nails toward the body, left forearm horizontal, elbows to the rear.

At the command *march* raise the left leg to the front, bending and elevating the knee as much as possible, that part of the leg between the knee and instep vertical, the toe depressed; replace the foot in its former position and execute the same movement with the right leg.

The cadence, one hundred and eighty steps per minute, is indicated by the instructor who counts *one*, *two*, as the feet are successively brought to the ground, commencing in common time and gradually increasing to double time. At the command, 1. *Knights*, 2. HALT, bring back the foot that is raised to the side of the other, and resume the position of a Knight in ranks.

1. *Forward.* 2. *Double time.* 3. MARCH.

At the first command throw the weight of the body on the right leg; at the second command raise the hands and arms as before explained; at the command *march* carry forward the left foot, the leg slightly bent knee somewhat raised and plant the foot, toe first, thirty-five inches from the right, and so with the right foot, allowing a natural swinging motion of the arms.

Breathe as much as possible through the nose.

To halt, the command is: 1. *Knights.* 2. HALT.

To pass to *quick time* the command is: 1. *Quick time.* 2. MARCH. At the command *march*, plant the foot that is coming to the ground drop the hands to the side, advance the other foot in *quick time* and plant it thirty inches from the one in rear, resuming, or taking up the march in quick time.

1. *By file.* 2. (*Right* or *left*). 3. DRESS. 4. FRONT.

Place two Knights abreast, two or more yards in advance, to establish the line; at the command *dress* the others move up successively in *quick time*, until about six inches behind the alignment; each then moves on the line, which should never be passed, taking steps of two or three inches, casting the eyes to the right as before explained, keeping the shoulders square to the front and, without opening his arms, touches with his elbow the Knight on his right.

At the command *front* the habitual position is promptly resumed without jerk.

1. *Right* (or *left*). 2. DRESS. 3. FRONT.

At the command *dress*, the entire rank, except the Knight established as a basis, moves forward and dresses up to the line, as before explained. The instructor verifies the alignment, by placing himself about two yards from the right flank, facing to the left, orders forward or backward such files as may be in rear or advance of the line, and commands *front*.

The whole movement should be promptly executed, and no delays be made in alignments.

1. *Right* (or *left*) *backward.* 2. DRESS. 3. FRONT.

March backward, and together, until six inches in rear of the line and then dress up, by short steps, as explained.

SCHOOL OF THE KNIGHT.

1. *Forward.* 2. *Guide* (*right* or *left*). 3. MARCH.

At the third command step off smartly with the left foot, the guide marching straight to the front To do this he must take points in advance, perpendicular to the line, and with the greatest care observe the length and cadence of the steps.

The instructor observes that the Knights touch lightly the elbow toward the side of the guide; that they do not open out either arm; that they yield to pressure coming from the side of the guide and resist pressure coming from the opposite direction; that by shortening or lengthening the steps they gradually recover the alignment and touch of elbow if lost; and that they keep the head and shoulders square to the front; that the guide takes the full step and cadence; that the principles of the step as before explained are carefully observed, in the most minute detail, and that the hands and arms are kept in their proper position, easy and all alike, but without unauthorized oscillation.

1. *Right* (or *left*). 2. FACE 3 *Forward.* 4. MARCH.

Being at a halt; face to the right and march as before.

1. *By the right* (or *left*) *flank.* 2. MARCH.

Being in march. The command *march* is given as the right foot strikes the ground; advance and plant the left foot at full distance, then turn to the right and step off in the new direction with the right foot. To march by the *left flank* apply the general rule, page 10.

In marching in column of files, the Knights cover each other; *keep closed to facing distance* and avoid spreading the feet and legs apart. Observe that this movement is similar to *right* (or *left*) *face* except that it is executed in march.

It is habitually executed in *quick time;* but if necessary to march in *double time,* the distance is increased to 21 inches.

1. *Column right* (or *left*). 2. March.

Being in march. At the command *march* the leading file turns half to the right,—that is, at an angle of forty-five degrees,—advances one step, and again turning half right, continues the march at right angles with the former direction; thus by two steps describing the arc of a small circle The other files keep closed up to proper distance and follow in his trace.

1. *Column half right* (or *left*). 2. March.

Is similarly executed.

1. *Forward.* 2. *Column right* (or *left*). 3 March; or 1. *Forward,* 2. *Column half right* (or *left*).
3. March,

Puts a column of files in motion and changes its direction.

1. *Knights.* 2. Halt,

Is the command to halt a column of files; and

1. *Left* (or *right*). 2. Face,

To face it to the front.

1. *By the left* (or *right*) *flank.* 2. March.
3. *Guide* (*left* or *right*),

Is given when marching in column of files to march in line; or when marching in line, to march in column of files. In the latter case, omit the third command.

SCHOOL OF THE KNIGHT.

1. *Right* (or *left*) *Oblique.* 2. MARCH.

Being in line marching. At the second command each Knight makes a half face to the right and marches straight in the new direction. As they no long. r touch elbows they glance along the shoulders of the nearest files toward the side of the guide, being that to which they are obliquing, and regulate their steps so that their shoulders are always behind those of the next Knight on that side, and that his head conceals the heads of the others in the rank The same length of step and same degree of obliquity is preserved, the line of the rank remaining parallel to its original position.

This being a half flank it is better to give the second command as the right foot strikes the ground, and execute the movement in a manner similar to the *right* (or *left*) *flank*, but it is not deemed absolutely essential.

To resume the original direction, command: 1 *Forward.* 2. MARCH. The guide is then on the side where it was previous to obliquing.

If at a *halt*, the Knights half face to the right at the first command and step off at the command *march*.

If halted while obliquing, they will halt, pause one cadence of a minute, and face to the front without further command

The guide is always on the side towards which the oblique is made; on resuming the direct march the guide is on the side where it was previous to the oblique, without any indication to that effect being given.

In *column of files* oblique by the same commands and means as when in line, the leading file being the guide.

WHEELINGS

Are of two kinds; on fixed, and on movable pivots.

These are important movements, and each Knight should be required successively to act as pivot, and to conduct the marching flank. The wheelings should also be repeated in double time as soon as the squad is able to execute them properly in quick time.

The fixed pivot—from a halt.

1. *In circle, right* (or *left*) *wheel.* 2. MARCH.

At the command *march* all, except the pivot, step off with the left foot, at the same time turning the heads a little to the left, the eyes fixed on the eyes of the Knights to the left; the pivot Knight marks time in his place, gradually turning his body to conform to the movements of the marching flank. The one who conducts the marching flank takes steps of thirty inches, and from the first step advances the left shoulder a little, casts his eyes along the rank, and feels lightly the elbow of the next one toward the pivot, but never pushes him. Each of the others lengthens the step in proportion to the distance from the pivot, touches with the elbow toward it and resists pressure from the opposite side, conforms to the movement of the marching flank, and maintains the alignment. After wheeling around the circle several times command: 1 *Knights.* 2 HALT, when all stop and no one stirs. Now point out the defects and mistakes, then command: 1. *Left.* 2 DRESS. 3. FRONT.

1. *Right* (or *left*) *wheel.* 2 MARCH. 3. *Knights.* 4 HALT. 5. *Left* (or *right*). 6 DRESS. 7. FRONT.

Being at a halt, the squad wheels as before on a fixed pivot. At the fourth command, given when the squad is nearly at right angles with its original position, the line halts. After pointing out the defects, the instructor immediately dresses the line up to the perpendicular by the fifth and sixth commands; when done he commands *front.*

To wheel the squad and move it forward, command:

1. *Right* (or *left*) *wheel.* 2. MARCH. 3. *Forward.*
4. MARCH. 5. *Guide* (*right* or *left*).

The third command is given in time to add *march* the instant the wheel (one-fourth of a circle) is completed, when they march in the new direction, taking the guide as indicated.

1. *Right* (or *left*) *about.* 2. MARCH. 3. *Knights.*
4. HALT. 5. *Left* (or *right*). 6. DRESS. 7. FRONT.
Or, 3. *Forward.* 4. MARCH. 5. *Guide* (*right* or *left*).

This wheels the squad in a half circle to the right; when completed the squad is halted or moved, as explained before

Wheeling on a Movable Pivot.

The wheelings are made by the same commands and means as on a fixed pivot, except that the pivot takes steps of nine inches and thus gains ground forward, describing a small curve so as to clear the wheeling point. The curve is increased in size proportionately with the size of the squad or subdivision, and is equal to about one-half of the front of the squad or subdivision.

The command *forward* is given in time to add *march* the instant the wheel (one-fourth of a circle) is completed, at which all retake the thirty inch step, turn their heads square to the front and march straight forward. The squad may be halted by the same commands and means as before explained.

In wheeling on a movable pivot in double time, the pivot takes steps of eleven inches and the curve is augmented.

During the wheel the guide is upon the marching flank, and upon the completion of the wheel is upon the same flank that it was before the wheel was commenced, without any indication to that effect.

1. *Left* (or *right*) *turn*. 2. MARCH

Being in march.

The first command is given when the rank is three yards from the turning point.

At the command *march*, pronounced the instant the rank is to turn, the Knight on the left, who becomes the guide, faces to the left in marching (that is, executes *by the left flank* in his own person), and moves forward in the new direction without changing the cadence or length of the step. The others advance the shoulders opposite the guide, take the *double time* and advance in the new direction till they come successively on the allignment, then retake the step and cadence from the guide and dress toward him.

In turning in *double time* those on the side opposite the guide increase the gait in order to come into line.

While this movement should be well learned, the wheel will in nearly all cases effect the desired change of direction.

DOUBLE RANK.

The movements should now be repeated, the Knights being in double rank.

The distance between the ranks is *facing distance;* but on rough ground or when marching in double time it is increased to twenty-one inches. Upon halting, the rear rank closes up to facing distance

If marching in column of files each rear rank Knight dresses upon his front rank frater, who is guide of the file.

In changing direction in column of files each file wheels on a movable pivot.

In obliquing each rear rank Knight follows the one next on the right or left of his front rank frater.

Small commanderies, or less than forty-eight in line, ought not ordinarily to march in double rank.*

If there is but one Knight in the rear rank of the three on the left of the line he covers number *one* of the front rank; if there are but two in the rear rank of the left three, they cover numbers *one* and *three* of the front rank.

---

*A recommendation only.

Manual of the Sword.

Remarks. The rate of swiftness, or time occupied in the execution of each motion, is one-ninetieth of a minute. But in march the cadence of motion is changed to conform to the time indicated by the left foot, thus: The command of execution is given as the left foot is coming to the ground, and the first motion is commenced the instant the left foot is planted; the second motion is commenced the instant the left foot strikes the ground the second time, and so on.

If the sword is grasped too near the guards, or cross, the sword manual is rendered difficult and awkward. Ease and grace of movement in handling the sword can only be acquired by practice, therefore when the principles and motions are understood the Knights should frequently practice the manual by themselves This rule applies as well to the steps, cadence and facings as to the manual.

Avoid the common error of bowing when executing the manual; habitually maintain the erect position.

In the *double step*, being at a carry, at the command *double time*, carry the sword straight to the front, the blade vertical, the hand firmly grasping the hilt. the right forearm horizontal, elbow close to the body; if the sword is *at a right shoulder* or *port* it may so remain, but resume the *carry* after halting without command, observing the cadence of the step—that is, halt, pause one cadence of the step then carry swords When part of the commandery executes double time, the manual is executed by those only who increased the cadence.

It is better not to *draw swords* until ranks are formed and to *return* swords before the command: *break ranks*.

Correctness in detail is of the first importance, therefore each motion should be explained and executed separately, without especial regard to the cadence, until the details are understood To this end (for example) command: 1. By the numbers, 2. Swords, 3. Port. 4. Two. At the third command the *first motion* of the movement is executed. The instructor corrects the errors, commands *Two*, and the second motion is executed. The rapidity is gradually increased until the cadence is acquired. When the command *by the numbers* is given it is not repeated, but every succeeding command in the manual is executed with the numbers until the command *without the numbers* is given, or some foot movement intervenes.

Draw.

The manual should be learned first *by the numbers*, then alternated with and without the numbers, in order to attain the proper cadence and to become proficient in the mechanism.

1. *Draw.* 2. Swords.

First motion. At the command *swords*, seize the scabbard near the top, press it against the thigh with the left and grasp the handle with the right hand, at the same time bring the hilt a little forward, and draw the sword until the right forearm is horizontal.

MANUAL OF THE SWORD.

Second motion. Draw the sword quickly, raising the arm to its full extent, at an angle of forty-five degrees, point of sword toward the mouth of the scabbard.

Third motion. Turn the sword and bring it to a *present.* q. v.

Fourth motion. Bring the sword-blade vertically back against the right shoulder, edge of the sword to the front, thumb and forefingers embracing the grip, the left side of the grip and the thumb against the thigh, arm nearly extended, the other fingers extended and joined in the rear of the grip, elbow near the body, drop the left hand to the side. *This is the position of carry swords.*

If in two ranks, the rear rank takes two backward steps at the command *draw*, and after executing the fourth motion, pauses one ninetieth of a minute and steps back to its position.

1. *Present.* 2. Swords

Being at a carry, at the second command bring the sword vertically to the front, raising the hand so that the top of the cross hilt is on a line with the lower part of the chin, and about six inches from it, back of the hand to the front, the right forearm resting along the side and breast, elbow close to the body, helmet of the sword nearly against the breast, the thumb on the back of grip to the right, the blade inclined upward to the front at an angle of about sixty-five degrees.

Carry.

For Officers. At the command *present,* carry the sword to the position just indicated. At the command *swords* drop the point of the sword near the ground and on a

MANUAL OF THE SWORD.

Present.

Present.

Salute.

line with the right foot, extending the arm so that the right hand may be brought near to the right thigh, back of the hand to the rear, arm extended, flat of the blade to the front (This does not apply to past officers, the *Secretary, Treasurer,* or *standard guard.*) It is sometimes referred to as a *salute* or *Officers' present,* to distinguish it from the present of those who are not officers

For the standard. (The standard bearer habitually carries the heel of the staff supported at the right hip; the right hand grasping the staff at the height of the shoulder.) At the command *present* slip the right hand along the staff to the height of the eye; at the command *swords* lower the staff by straightening the arm to its full extent, the heel of the staff remaining at the hip. At *carry swords* bring back the standard to its habitual place.

Salutes in march by officers and standards are commenced when six yards from the person to be saluted, and cease when six yards past. In saluting, officers turn their heads and look toward the person being saluted simultaneous with the second motion.

Knights in the ranks do not salute, but retain the *carry* when in march.

Desiring to cause all to present swords as officers

the command is: 1. *Officers present* 2. Swords, which is executed as before explained.

1. *Carry.* 2. Swords.

From *present* At the second command bring the sword back to the position of *carry swords.* Avoid carrying the hand to the front and point of the sword to the rear of the shoulder in executing this motion.

1. *Support.* 2. Swords

First motion. Seize the blade at the right shoulder with the thumb and first three fingers of the left hand. *Second motion.* Carry the sword vertically in front of the body, with both hands, to the left side, edge of the blade to the front; the guard on a level with the hollow of the left elbow; right hand holding the grip; left elbow down; thumb and fingers of the left hand holding the blade vertical, pressed against the hollow of the left shoulder. *Third motion.* Carry the left hand to the right elbow, the left forearm resting over the right forearm, thumb over and supported by the right arm, the cross (guard) resting on the left arm near the elbow.

Support.

1. *Carry.* 2. Swords.

First motion. Seize the blade, without deranging its position, with the thumb and forefinger of the left hand, left elbow remaining close to the body, as a pivot.

Second motion. Carry the sword vertically with both hands to its place at a *carry*, fingers extended, pressing the sword gently against the hollow of the shoulder, hand at the height of the shoulder, its back to the front, elbow near the body.

Third motion Drop the left hand to the side.

MANUAL OF THE SWORD.

1. *Swords*. 2 Port.

Swords Port.

First motion. Seize the blade at the shoulder with the left hand

Second motion. Bring the sword diagonally across the front of the body, flat of the blade to the front and resting in the left hand at the height of the breast, thumb extended in rear along the blade toward the point, the right hand grasping the hilt and nearly in front of the right hip, edge of the sword down.

1. *Carry*. 2. Swords.

First motion. Bring back the sword with both hands, the left hand as high as the right armpit, pressing the blade to its place, fingers extended at the height of the shoulder, elbow near the body, back of hand to the front.

Second motion. Drop the left hand to the side.

1. *Order*. 2. Swords.

Drop the sword-point to the ground about an inch from the point of the right toe and on a line with the toes; sword vertical, the right hand resting on the helmet, back of the hand up, first three fingers in front touching the grip, the thumb and little finger partially embracing it.

1. *Carry*. 2. Swords.

Bring the sword back to its position in *carry*. Order.

Charge.

1 *With sword.* **2 Charge.**

Execute the first motion of *about face*, except that the right heel is in rear of the left; bend the left knee a little, inclining the body forward, the weight principally on the left foot, at the same time drop the point of the sword forward to the height of the belt, the right hand firmly grasping the handle, thumb against the hip (This can also be executed in march, the shoulders being kept square to the front.)

1. *Carry.* **2. Swords.**

Face to the front and resume the position of *carry swords*.

1. *Right shoulder.* **2. Swords.**

Bring the flat of the sword upon the right shoulder, guard as high as the armpit, thumb nearly touching the side of the right breast, point of the sword up to the left and rear so as to clear the chapeau.

1. *Carry.* **2. Swords.**

Resume that position.

1. *Support.* **2 Swords.**

The sword being at a *right shoulder.*

First motion. Lower the sword to a *carry*

Second motion. Seize the blade as described on page 32.

Third motion. Carry the sword to the left side, as described on page 32.

Fourth motion. Drop the left hand to the side.

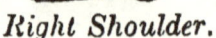

Right Shoulder.

1. *Carry.* 2. Swords.

After *support swords.*

1. *Rear rest.* 2 Swords.

First motion. Execute the *right shoulder swords*, as explained.

Second motion. Drop the sword-point to the left and rear and let the blade rest across the shoulders in rear of the neck, at same time raise the left hand, palm to the front, and grasp the blade near the shoulder with the fingers and thumb, holding the grip in like manner with the fingers and thumb of the right hand, elbows close to the body. Care should be taken not to derange the position of the head and shoulders in executing this movement.

Rear Rest.

1. *Carry.* 2 Swords.

First motion. Drop the left hand to the side and come to the position of *right shoulder swords.*

Second motion. Resume the carry.

1. *Reverse.* 2. Swords.

First motion. Raise and carry the sword vertically to the front, the elbow advanced and forming an obtuse angle.

Second motion. Bring the point down to the front and rear, turning the sword by a wrist movement completely around, so that the edge will be down and the blade inclined to the rear at an angle of forty five degrees, at the same time carry the left forearm horizontally behind the

1st motion, Reverse.

back, the left hand palm out, clasping the blade; support the sword with the elbow against the right side, assisted by the left hand in rear; holding the grip with the thumb and forefinger of the right hand, the other fingers successively more curved, the guards (cross) nearly against the shoulder.

1. *Carry*. 2. SWORDS.

First motion. Retake the first position of *reverse* by inverse means. *Second motion*. Resume the carry.

Reverse. 1. *Sword arm*. 2. REST.

Bring the right hand in front of the body, arm extended, blade resting along the right forearm and diagonally across the body, embrace the back of the right hand with the palm of the left. Resume the carry at that command.

1. *Parade*, 2. REST.

First motion. Carry the right foot three inches to the rear, the left knee slightly bent, resting the weight of the body principally on the right foot. *Second motion*. Drop the sword-point to the ground to the right and on a line with the great toe of the left foot parallel to the front; the sword vertical in front of the center of the body; fingers and thumb holding the helmet, which rests in the palm of the right hand, back of the hand up embraced and covered by the left hand

Sword-arm Rest.

Parade Rest.

MANUAL OF THE SWORD. 37

Being at Parade Rest. 1. *Rest on.* 2. Swords.

Incline the head to the front. At the command *Knights,* raise the head.

1. *Knights* (or *Commandery*). 2 Attention. 2. *Carry.* 4 Swords.

At the second command bring the right foot to the side of the left, body erect in *position,* drop the left hand to the side, the right hand hanging naturally at the side and holding the grip, sword-blade inclining across in front of right leg, the sword-point undisturbed. At the fourth command bring the sword to a carry.

1. *From right open files.* 2 March.

At the first command all except the Knight on the right, who stands at a carry, turn the heads and drop the sword point to the right, hand at the right breast, sword horizontal. At the command *march* they take the left side step, all stepping together, until each in succession has gained such an interval that the sword-point will touch the left arm of the Knight on the right observing that the alignment is preserved; as each gains this interval he turns the head to the front and resumes the carry.

Right open files.

1. *From left open files.* 2. March.

Is similarly executed, except that the right hand is at the left breast, guards in front of the left arm, the sword horizontal to the left in prolongation of the right forearm.

MANUAL OF THE SWORD.

1. *From right and left open files*
2. MARCH.

Causes the lines to take intervals right and left simultaneously from the designated flank or file indicated.

1. *Right* (or *left*). 2. FACE. 3. *Close files.* 4. MARCH.

At the fourth command the Knight in front faces to the left; the others close up in quick time and successively face to the left, dress to the right, and immediately turn the head to the front.

Left open files.

1. *Cross.* 2. SWORDS

The lines being fully two yards apart and facing each other.

First motion. Bring the sword to a *present.* Second motion. Plant the right foot 16 inches straight to the front, right knee s l i g h t l y bent, at the same time raising the right hand, arm extended, wrist

Cross Swords.

MANUAL OF THE SWORD.

as high as the head, sword in prolongation of the arm, thumb extended along the left of the grip, back of sword up; cross the swords six inches from their points with the Knight opposite, at the same instant plant the foot with very light shock.

1. *Carry.* 2. SWORDS.

First motion. Bring back the foot to its former place and the sword to a present. *Second motion.* Resume the carry.

1. *Knights.* 2. KNEEL

Being at *parade rest.*

First motion. Carry the right foot about twenty-eight inches to the rear.

Second motion. Kneel on the right knee so that its front and the rear of the left heel will be on a line parallel with the front; head erect.

1. *Rest on.* 2. SWORDS.

Incline the head to the front

Kneeling, rest on.

1. *Knights.* 2. RISE

At the first command raise the head. At the second command, rise. *Second motion.* Bring the right foot near to the left, resuming the position of *parade rest.*

1. *Knights.* 2. ATTENTION. 3. *Carry.* 4. SWORDS.
Resume that position.

1. *Knights.* 2. RETURN 3. SWORDS.

At the command *return*, seize the scabbard with the left hand, near the top, inclining it a little forward, and bring the sword about six inches in front of the left shoul-

der, blade vertical, lower part of the hand at the height of the chin. *Second motion.* Lower the blade across and along the left arm, the point to the rear; turn the head slightly to the left, fixing the eyes on the opening of the scabbard, and insert the blade, assisted by the thumb and forefinger of the left hand, until the right forearm is horizontal. At the command *swords* return the blade, turn the head to the front and drop the hands to the sides. (The second motion should occupy the time of three motions.) If *in two ranks*, at the command *return* the rear rank takes two backward steps, and resumes its place after the execution of the command *swords*.

Return.

1. *Secure.* 2. SWORDS.

The sword being in the scabbard.

First motion. At the command *swords* seize the scabbard with the left hand, palm front, thumb to the left, arm extended. *Second motion.* Raise the sword, in the scabbard, bring the left hand in front and nearly as high as the belt and a little to the left of the buckles the sword, in the scabbard, resting along the left forearm, back of the hand down, the cross at the hollow of the elbow.

Secure.

1. *Drop.* 2. SWORDS.

Lower the Sword (in the scabbard) to its place.

MANUAL OF THE SWORD. 41

1. *Inspection.* 2. SWORDS.

First motion. Come to a present. *Second motion.* Turn the wrist outward to show the other side of the blade, pause one cadence, and turn the wrist back. *Third motion.* Resume the carry. [Executed successively as inspector approaches.]

For the Chapeau or Cap.

1. *Knights* (or *Commandery*). 2. UN-COVER.*

First motion. Take the chapeau (or cap) by the front piece with the left hand. *Second motion.* Raise the chapeau and place it on the right shoulder, slightly inclined to the front, holding it in that position with the left hand.

1. *Knights* (or *Commandery*).
2. RE-COVER.*

First motion. Replace the chapeau (or cap) on the head. *Second motion.* Drop the hand to the side.

Uncover. Never execute the *uncover* unless the swords are sheathed, at an *order*, or (with the right hand) when at a *secure*. *To uncover and present at the same time is unmilitary and awkward.*

The *uncover* may be executed by signals, thus:

First motion. Extend the left hand in front of the breast, palm up, fingers extended. *Second motion.* Execute the first motion of *uncover.* *Third motion.* Execute the second motion of *uncover.*

---

* Dwell slightly on the first syllable

To recover by signals *First motion.* Slowly raise the chapeau from the shoulder and place it on the head. *Second motion.* Drop the hand to the side.

THE SILENT MANUAL.

When the foregoing has been well learned it may be executed, being at "open order" (*vide* School of the Commandery) at the commands:

1. *Continue the manual.* 2. *Present.* 3. Swords.

At the command *swords* the manual is executed in the following order, without pause, except that the regular cadence of motions is preserved throughout.

1. Present swords. 2. Carry, swords.
3. Officers present, swords. 4. " "
5. Support, swords. 6. " "
7. Swords, port. 8. " "
9. Order, swords. 10. " "
11. With swords, charge. 12. " "
13. Right shoulder, swords. 14. " "
15. Right shoulder, swords.
16. Support, swords. 17. " "
18. Rear rest, swords. 19. " "
20. Reverse, swords. 21. " "
22. Sword arm, rest. 23. " "
24. Front rank, about face. The rear rank files (by one side step, about eighteen inches, to the right, if it be single rank open order) cover the files in the front rank simultaneously with their *about face*.
25. Cross, swords. 26 Carry, swords.

MANUAL OF THE SWORD. 43

27. Front rank, about face. Rear rank re-covers intervals, by a side step to the left, at same instant with the *about face* of the front rank.
28. Parade rest
29. Knights, kneel.   30. Rest on swords.
31. Knights, rise.   32. Knights, attention.
33. Carry, swords.   34. Return swords.
35. Secure, swords.   36. Drop, swords.
 7. Knights, un cover.   38. Knights, re-cover.
 9. Right hand salute.   40. Left hand salute.
41. Draw, swords.
42. Parade rest. The *open files* is omitted

The whole of the *silent manual* occupies eighty-nine-tieths of a minute, including command.

Or 80 seconds, if seconds be the cadence A pause of one cadence may be made between each completed sword movement, if so instructed.

The Vice-Commanders stand at *order swords* during silent manual unless otherwise instructed.

THE SALUTES.

When addressed, face the Knight challenging; the inferior in rank then, if swords are drawn, salutes with it; this is acknowledged, and both resume the *carry* simultaneously, or the junior may stand at a *present* while making a short report.

If swords are not drawn the inferior in rank gives the *first motion* of the hand salute, which is acknowledged in full; the inferior in rank executes the *second* and *third motions*, so that the hands of both Knights may be dropped to the side at the same instant. The sword is never drawn to acknowledge a salute already given.

If the Chief is sitting he salutes with the hand, although his sword may be drawn. He does not rise to acknowledge salutes of an inferior in rank, but inferiors, when in the hall or in uniform, if not engaged in some particular duties arise when addressed by official superiors.

In passing a Knight, salute him with the hand farthest from him.

An officer or Knight mounted, dismounts before addressing official superiors not mounted.

School of the Officer.

Theory and practice should go hand in hand. Officers should be competent to take command in the absence of official superiors, and every one be able to command his subdivision with credit. A careless or ill informed officer may cause the best drilled commandery to appear at great disadvantage or throw it into confusion. An indolent manner of giving commands is demoralizing in its tendency; hence officers should be energetic and prompt and require every Knight to be equally prompt and attentive.

The idea that discipline can not be maintained among Knights of Honor is sheer nonsense, yet the instructor need not forget that his men are gentlemen who, out of ranks, are his peers.

An *officer's squad* should be organized, admitting as supernumeraries Knights who will take an interest in it and fill the place of absentees. Its members should be six or twelve beside its chief. Every member should be faithful and prompt in attendance, cheerfully obedient to orders, attentive and silent in ranks.

The chief of the squad, whether he be the Commander or some Knight selected for his peculiar fitness, must have absolute control. He indicates the lessons to be learned, commencing with the vocabulary and proceeds regularly through, without omitting anything. One of the most important requisites is promptness; therefore, havi g announced the lesson and the hour for meeting, the chief should himself be ready and, before the clock ceases to strike, command: FALL IN. He should always be prompt in time, prompt in giving and obeying orders, and prompt in the "etiquette of Knightly courtesy;" promptly meet, promptly commence and promptly dismiss the squad

After the oral lesson the squad should be drilled in it well and thoroughly, or better, as each motion is explained by a Knight, require its execution, until the principles are well understood.

Take frequent rests of two or three minutes only when discussion may be indulged in; but at the command *attention* conversation stops *instanter*. Discussion while under instruction should not be permitted; then the chief's *ipse dixit* is law final.

Perfect discipline should be observed from the first. It is quite as proper to talk during the conference of a degree as to talk during drill.

The officers should alternate in exercising a squad in the drill under supervision of the chief, whose criticisms should be for the benefit of all, not prosy, but clear cut, pointed explanations without circumlocution or unnecessary comment.

The instructor ought never to require a movement to be made until he has fully explained it, and sees that *no movement, however trivial it may appear, is performed carelessly or with undue haste.* He should practice the officers and guides especially in estimating distances and in becoming familiar with the bugle and sword signals. The *assembly, forward, halt* and *threes right* are particularly important when the Knights assemble in large numbers

By giving each frequent opportunities to command, errors may be corrected, uniformity secured, ambition to excel stimulated, closer attention and study encouraged and the general interest increased

All commands to men under arms are given with the sword drawn. If for any purpose Knights of Honor and troops are together, officers execute the first motion of *officers present* at the command *present*, and the second motion at the command *arms* (or *sabre*) and the Knights *present swords*. In like manner at the command *Fours right* (or *left*) *march*, Knights of Honor execute *Threes right* (or *left*) *march*. At the command *Platoons right wheel*, etc., Knights of Honor execute *Divisions* (or *double sections*) *right wheel*, and so on. At the command *parade rest* the Vice-Commanders and officers of higher rank take that position; at the command *attention* they *carry swords*.

When marching in double time officers who are in command, so that their position is in front or a yard or more from the flank, bring their swords to the position of *port*, steadying the scabbard with the left hand.

About face for officers. At the command *about* carry the toe of the right foot about eight inches to the rear and three inches to the left of the left heel, without deranging the direction of the left foot. At the command *face* turn to the right upon the left heel and right toe, face to the rear and replace the right heel by the side of the left.

If so directed, officers omit the manual except the *present, order, parade rest, rest on swords* and *uncover.*

THE BAND.

The Drum-major faces the band and gives the signal to *march*. His position is two yards in front of the center of the band.

The countermarch is executed by the file leaders to the right of the Drum-major wheeling individually about to the right, those to his left to the left; the other men of each file follow their file leaders. The Drum-major passes through the center

In executing *rear open order* each rank of the band steps back three yards from the rank in its front, the front being on a line with the front rank of the Commandery and six yards from its right.

Bands should be required to keep their proper distances and take the full thirty inch step, also that they should be careful to keep time with each other, when practicable; and, if near together, two should not play at the same time

At the command *halt* the music ceases.

Do not take it for granted that the band is familiar with the cadence in *common* and *quick time*, but test its accuracy by the watch and notice the length of the step.

School of the Commandery.

Remarks. Thorough instruction in the elementary School of the Knight is absolutely essential to success in the movements of the Commandery, which depend upon the precision of the drill. This can only be attained by *practice, the strictest attention of every Knight,* and the intelligent assistance of the chiefs of subdivisions. One awkward Knight or the undue swinging of a single hand, will wholly destroy the beauty of the line.

In this work "file closers" have been dispensed with, and officers are assigned places that will utilize every available uniform in extending the lines, because many Commanderies are small and comparatively few of their members are equipped, hence they can not afford to scatter their numerical strength, and because the necessity for file closers does not appear in the movements of a Commandery, as is claimed for the operations of belligerents, nor do they add to the symmetry of the formations for display.

The Past Officers wearing shoulder-straps form on the right according to height, but have no other distinction.

The Commander as instructor goes wherever his presence is necessary; in column his place is on the left of the First Vice-Commander, or four yards to the left and abreast of the leading subdivision; if the Commandery be in line his post is two yards in front of the center, or on the right flank at the right of the First Vice-Commander.

The First Vice-Commander, in line, is on the right flank; in column of divisions, as chief of the first division, he marches two yards in front of its center. He is also the right or left guide, according as in the maneuvers he finds himself on the right or left of the Commandery.

The Second Vice-Commander in line is, in like manner, on the left flank as *left guide*. He is chief of the rear division when the right is in front, and of the leading division when the left is in front.

It is the duty of the Vice-Commanders and Aides to assist the Commander in maintaining order in the ranks; habitually preserving their own correct position, and if necessary, they caution the Knights in a low tone.

The Secretary, Treasurer and Sentry having shoulder-straps, form with the *Past Officers;* or form the rear rank of the *Standard Guard,* when the formation is double rank.

The Senior Aide is on the right, and the Junior Aide on the left of the Standard Bearer or " Guard " These three form the Standard Guard, whose place is in the front rank, and as near the center of the Commandery as practicable.

A Commandery is divided into two, and if desirable into three or four (nearly) equal parts; each part is called a *division*, the odd number of threes being in the division on the left. It is better that there should be

but two divisions, so designated when the Commandery is formed. But for the purpose of placing the standard in a center division, there may be three, or in order to equally divide the Commandery into four parts, to form square when double sections will not accomplish it, four divisions may be formed. In line of three ranks the front rank is the *first division*, the middle rank is the *second division*, and the rear rank the *third division*.*
In column, the leading division is the *first division*, whether the right or left is in front.

The Chief of a subdivision is the officer or Knight on its right, unless otherwise especially designated.

The Guide of a subdivision is generally the Knight on its left.

Subdivisions are designated numerically from right to left, when in line, and from the head of the column to the rear. The designation changes when by facing, etc., the left becomes the right; officers in command caution *first division*, etc., whenever the designation is changed.

FORMATION OF A COMMANDERY.

At the sound of the *assembly* every Knight hastens to the place from which the sound came; *promptness* being the first most excellent quality for a well drilled Commandery. The First Vice-Commander commands:

FALL IN,

and indicates the basis for the line, be then places himself six yards in front of the center, facing it.

The Knights form in column of files faced to right, graduated in height from front to rear, tallest in front, swords at *carry*.

---

* This is a matter of convenience, not the rule.

SCHOOL OF THE COMMANDERY.

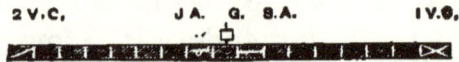

The First Vice-Commander now orders:

1. *Left.* 2. FACE. 3. COUNT THREES.

The First Knight on the right (front and rear rank) counts *one*, the next at his left says *two*, the next *three*, the next *one*, and so on to the left, without turning their heads, but counting in a firm, quick tone. Observing the cadence adds much to the appearance and effect.

[The First Vice-Commander may be counted as *one* in the leading three of very small Commanderies, and the Second Vice-Commander may march with the left three if the number is wanting.]

The First Vice Commander then commands: ONES COUNT, when numbers one of each three successively turn their heads to the left, at the same time count *one*, *two*, etc., from right to left, and immediately turn the head to the front. He then indicates the right and left of divisions, leaving the odd three in the left division, and commands:

1. *Second division.* 2. *Left side step.* 3. MARCH. 4. *Division.* 5. HALT.

The fifth command is given when the division has gained an interval of two yards.

In the meantime the Standard Guard (with the standard) forms six yards from the left, perpendicular to the line and in inverse order; that is, the Senior Aide is on the left and the Junior Aide on the right of the Standard Bearer (Guard).

SCHOOL OF THE COMMANDERY.

The First Vice Commander now commands:

1. *Standard Guard.* 2. POST. 3. *Present.* 4 SWORDS.

The line presents and the guard marches, under direction of the Senior Aide, standard saluting, between the Commandery and First Vice-Commander, opposite to its place, wheels to the right, marches through the opening between the divisions and halts, comes to an *about face,* and the First Vice Commander immediately commands:

1. *Carry.* 2. SWORDS. 3. *Right:* 4. DRESS. 5. FRONT. 6. *Present.* 7. SWORDS.

This is acknowledged by the Commander, who raises his chapeau, he having taken position three yards in rear of First Vice-Commander and facing the Commandery. He stands with arms folded until just before the command *present.*

The First Vice-Commander comes to an *about face,* salutes with the sword and says:

Sir, the Commandery is formed.

The salute is acknowledged with the hand and the First Vice Commander faces about, marches to within one yard of the line, turns to the left, and when opposite his place turns to the right and halts in rear of it, faces about and dresses on the line

When he faces the Commandery to the left into line (if so instructed) he brings it to *support swords* and calls the roll, each Knight coming to a *carry* and *order swords* as his name is called, and then answers, "Here."

This is the formal ceremony, but the Commander may, in emergencies, order the Commandery to *fall in;*

left face; count threes; ones count, and designate the divisions only.

If preferred, the order may be *count sixes,* in lieu of *threes.*

How to Determine Position in Column.

The odd threes are the right and the even threes the left of sections.

When *ones count,* the odd threes being the right and the even threes the left of sections, the number of each section and position of any three may be instantly ascertained by dividing the number by two, thus: the three whose number one counted "six" knows that, as the half of six is three, it is the left (even numbered) half of the third section, or sixth three from the right of the line or head of the column. If he counted "five," the three is the next or first three to the left (or rear) of the second section.

An odd three at the rear of the column marches in rear of the three on the side of the guide and of the rear section. The First Vice-Commander may take the place of number one on the right of the line and the Second Vice-Commander may march as the left flank man, in which case they temporarily lose their identity as officers and become Knights in rank to fill vacancies.

If there are but two in the three on the left, number two marches, when in column, as number three, leaving the place of number two vacant, but in line he dresses up to his number one.

It is not necessary to *count twos* for any purpose, though it may be done if desired.

To *count sixes* in lieu of threes is perhaps the simplest method to determine positions in line and column for all possible combinations of successive movements.

To Form in Two Ranks.

The Knights *fall in* as explained; the Commander commands:

1. *In two ranks form Commandery.* 2. MARCH.

At the second command the First Vice-Commander and the Knight on the right face to the left (front). The Second Knight places himself in rear covering the first one, the others close in quick time, form alternately in front and rear rank, and each faces to the front upon arriving in his proper place; then *count threes* as before explained. Or the Knights may fall in, if so instructed, in two ranks, faced to the right, and the formation is completed as before.

To Dismiss the Commandery.

Being in line at a halt.

1. *Return.* 2. SWORDS. 3. *Break ranks.* 4. MARCH.

To Open Ranks.

Being at a halt.

1. *Rear open order.* 2. MARCH 3. FRONT.

At the first command the First Vice Commander and Second Vice-Commander march backward three yards to mark the new alignment. At the command *march* the front rank dresses to the right, the rear rank casts the eyes to the right and steps backward, halts a little in rear of alignment and dresses to the right on the line established by the Vice Commanders. The Commander verifies the alignment of the front and the First

Vice-Commander of the rear ranks At the command *front* the Vice Commanders place themselves three yards in front of the centers of their divisions.

1. *Close order.* 2. MARCH.

At the command *march* the officers face about, approach to within one yard of the line, march along its front and resume their places in line, the rear rank closes up in quick time to facing distance, each Knight covering his front rank frater.

In Line, Single Rank, to Open Order.

The same rules and commands apply as in double rank, except that *twos* are counted, if not otherwise known; the even numbers march straight backward and form the rear rank, in open order, so as to be exactly in rear of their own intervals between numbers *one* of the front rank. The intervals are not closed in dressing.

When ranks are closed they resume their places in line.

To March in Line.

1. *Forward.* 2. *Guide right* (or *left*). 3. MARCH.

At the command *march* all step off with the left foot in quick time, the First Vice-Commander as right guide taking points in advance perpendicular to the line, and with the greatest care observes the length and cadence of the steps. The touch of elbow toward the guide is kept up and the alignment carefully preserved This should be frequently practiced, and for long distances.

1. *Commandery.* 2. HALT.

At the second command every Knight halts and the alignment is made

To Wheel the Commandery.

Being in line at halt:

1. *Right* (or *left*) *wheel*. 2. MARCH. 3. *Commandery*.
4. HALT. 5. *Left* (or *right*). 6 DRESS. 7. FRONT.

At the command *march* the commandery wheels to right on a fixed pivot. The First Vice Commander stands fast, so that the breast of the pivot Knight may rest against his left arm at the completion of the wheel. The Commander superintends the wheel, moves by the shortest line to a point, commandery distance, where the left of the line will rest directly in front of the First Vice Commander and facing him. At the command *halt*, given when the left guide is three yards from the perpendicular, the Commandery halts and the Second Vice-Commander promptly places himself so that his breast will touch the Commander's right arm, who steps back two yards and commands *left*, DRESS, when the Knights dress up to the line of the pivot and Second Vice-Commander. At the command *front* the First Vice Commander places himself on the right of the pivot.

To *continue the march* upon completion of the wheel the Commander Commands *forward* when the Second Vice-Commander arrives at three yards from the perpendicular, adding MARCH the instant the wheel is completed, and *guide left* (or *right*) immediately afterward. At the command *forward* the First Vice-Commander places himself at the side of the pivot

In all wheels the guide is on the marching flank and slightly advances the shoulder opposite the pivot, keeping the pivot constantly in view.

In wheeling on a movable pivot the command *forward* is given in time to add *march* the instant the wheel is completed, and the guide is announced on either flank.

To *continue the wheel* that caution is given, as the marching flank approaches the perpendicular, and the wheeling is kept up as if but just commenced. If on a fixed pivot, the Vice Commander on the pivot flank places himself in line, at the side of the pivot Knight, and halts as before. This may be continued *ad libitum*, or the direction of the wheel may be changed at the command: 1 *Left* (or *right*) *wheel*. 2. MARCH, when the same principles will govern as before.

To Effect a Slight Change of Direction.

Incline to the right (or *left*).

Being in march.

The guide advances gradually the left shoulder and marches in the new direction; all the files advance the left shoulder and conform to the movements of the guide, lengthening or shortening the step according as the change is toward the side of the guide or the side opposite.

While this should be learned, a half wheel will ordinarily effect the desired object.

To Turn.

1. *Right* (or *left*) *turn*. 2 MARCH.

Is given when marching in line.

At the second command the First Vice-Commander faces to the right, without halting, and continues the march; all the files increase the gait and hasten to his left, taking the step and touch of elbow from him on arriving in line

Right (or *left*) *half turn* is similarly executed.

SCHOOL OF THE COMMANDERY.

To March by the Flank.

Being in line at a halt.
1. *Right* (or *left*). 2. FACE. 3. *Forward.* 4. MARCH. Or, 1. *By the right* (or *left*) *flank.* 2. MARCH, if in march. Or, from a halt or in march command:

1. *Threes right* (or *left*). 2. MARCH.

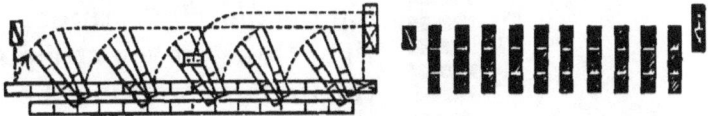

At the command *march* each three wheels to the rig't on a fixed pivot. Upon completion of the wheel the front rank of each three takes the full step, the rear ranks fall back until there are twenty one inches between the front and rear ranks. The front rank of the second three will be twenty-one inches from the rear rank of the first three, and so on to the rear of the column.

The Vice Commanders each march forty-four inches to the front and face to the right; the First Vice-Commander places himself twenty one inches in front of the left file of the first three, and marches on a line parallel to the former front of the commandery, and the Second Vice Commander follows twenty-one inches in rear of the left file of the last three. This brings the front rank of each three at wheeling distance, as they would be had there been but one rank in the line; the rear ranks are half way between the front ranks of the threes

In wheeling by threes the *forward march* is always taken up on completion of the wheel unless the command to *halt* is given.

To March in Columns of Threes to the Front.

Being in line, at a halt or in march.

1. *Right* (or *left*) *forward.* 2. *Threes right* (or *left*).
3. MARCH.

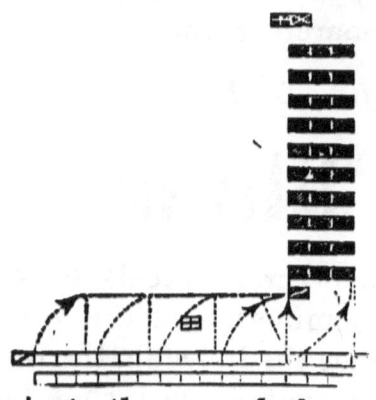

At the third command the First Vice-Commander places himself in front of the left file of the right three; the right three moves straight to the front, shortening the first three steps; the rear rank, if there be one, falls back to halt distance; the other threes wheel to the right on a fixed pivot; the second three, when its wheel is two-thirds completed, wheels to the left on a movable pivot and follows the first three, and the others, having wheeled to the right, move forward and wheel to the left on the same ground as the second.

To Change Direction of Column.

Being in march.

1. *Column right* (or *left*). 2. MARCH.

If the change of direction be to the side opposite the guide, he wheels as if on the marching flank of a rank of three: if the change of direction be toward the side of the guide, he shortens his steps at the command *march* and wheels to the right, the leading three wheels on a movable pivot, its pivot following the trace of the guide. The wheel being completed the guide and leading rank retake the thirty inch step; the other threes move forward and wheel on the same ground.

SCHOOL OF THE COMMANDERY.

1. *Column half right* (or *left*). 2. March, is similarly executed.

1. *Forward.* 2. *Column right* (or *left*). 3. March. Puts the column in march and changes its direction.

1. *Threes right* (or *left*). 2. *Column right* (or *left*).
3. March,

Forms column and changes its direction.

To Halt a Column and to Put it in Motion.

1. *Commandery.* 2. Halt. Or, 1. *Forward.* 2. March.

To Oblique in Column.

In obliquing in column of threes or subdivisions, the guide, without indication, is always on the side toward which the oblique is made. On resuming the direct march the guide, without indication, is on the same side it was previous to the oblique.

Practice obliquing in column and in line often and for a long distance at a time, that the errors may be seen and corrected.

1. *Right* (or *left*) *oblique.** 2 March.

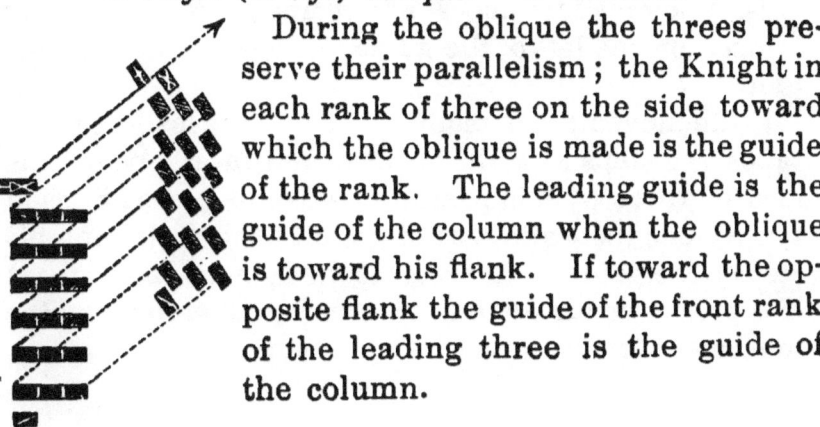

During the oblique the threes preserve their parallelism; the Knight in each rank of three on the side toward which the oblique is made is the guide of the rank. The leading guide is the guide of the column when the oblique is toward his flank. If toward the opposite flank the guide of the front rank of the leading three is the guide of the column.

*Pronounced Obe-like.

1. *Forward.* 2. March

Is given to resume the direct march.

To March a Column of Threes to the Rear.

1. *Threes right* (or *left*) *about.* 2. March.

Each rank of three wheels about on a fixed pivot and marches to the former rear. The rear ranks, if there are two ranks, preserve their distance of twenty-one inches from the front ranks when in column of threes; the pivot of the rear rank closes up to his front rank pivot, covers him during the wheel, and on its completion falls back to twenty-one inches.

The guide at the head of the column takes two steps forward, faces to the right, and places himself, on completion of the about, in rear of the file on the marching flank of the now rear three. The guide at the rear of the column faces to the right and places himself, on completion of the about, in front of the file on the marching flank of the now leading three.

The Commander faces about and hastens to place himself on the left of the guide at the head of the column.

If the movement is made to the left, the leading guide takes two steps straight forward and faces about; the leading three wheels past him, when he places himself twenty-one inches in rear of its left file by retracing his steps; the guide in the rear of the column faces about and preserves his distance, marching forward when the movement is completed.

To Form Line from Column of Threes.

1. *Threes right* (or *left*). 2. March. 3. *Guide* (*right* or *left*); or, 3. *Commandery*. 4. Halt. 5. *Left* (or *right*). 6. Dress. 7. Front.

The threes wheel to the right, into line, on a fixed pivot.

If in two ranks the rear rank closes to facing distance during the wheel, and if executed in *double time*, regains the distance of twenty-one inches should the line advance when formed. The guide, if in front of the pivot, takes two steps forward and faces to the right, placing himself on the left of the leading three upon completion of the wheel. If in front of the marching flank, he wheels to the right with the leading three, obliquing at the same time so as to uncover the file, and places himself on the left of the file when the wheel is completed. The guide in rear takes his place on the right of the Commandery, and the guide is announced the instant the threes unite in line.

If the command to *halt* be given as the threes wheel into line, the Commander places the leading guide on the line of the pivots at sufficient distance to admit the late leading three which dresses on the guide, the others dress up to the pivot of the three late in its front, thus insuring a prompt alignment.

1. *On right* (or *left*) *into line*. 2. March. 3. *Commandery*. 4. Halt. 5. *Right* (or *left*). 6. Dress. 7. Front.

At the command *march* the leading three wheels to the right on a movable pivot, and moves forward dressing on the guide who places himself on its right and conducts it. The other threes march a distance equal

64   SCHOOL OF THE COMMANDERY.

to their fronts beyond the wheeling point of the three next preceding, wheel to the right and advance as did the first three. The rear guide places himself on the left of the rear three as it wheels to the right.

At the command *halt,* given when the leading three has advanced commandery distance in the new direction, or at a less distance if desired by the Commander, it halts, and at the sixth command, given immediately

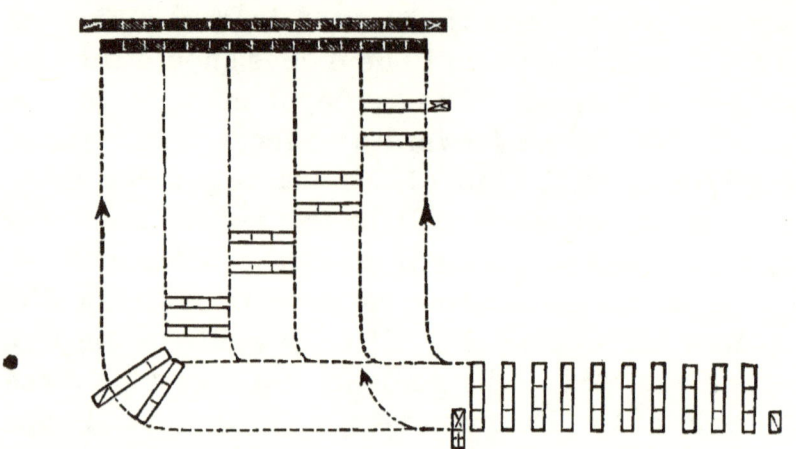

after, dresses to the right. The other threes halt and dress successively on arriving in line. The rear rank, if there is one, closes to facing distance upon halting.

The seventh command is given when the last three has dressed.

If in double rank, and it is desired to form line in single rank, precede the first command by, 1. *In single rank.* 2. *On right into line,* etc., and the rear ranks execute the movement the same as the others, passing a distance equal to their front beyond where their front ranks commenced the wheel.

If in single rank, to *form in double rank* the command

is, 1. *In double rank.* 2. *On right into line,* etc. The movement is similar. The rear rank of each three wheels to the right on the same ground as its front rank.

If marching in double time, or in *quick time* and the command be *double time,* the Commander orders: *guide right,* when the leading three has wheeled out of the column; it then advances in quick time; the others continue the double time until they successively arrive in line when they take the step and alignment from the guide.

Front into Line in Single and Double Rank.

1. *Right* (or *left*) *front into line.* 2. March. 3. *Commandery.* 4. Halt. 5. *Left* (or *right*). 6. Dress. 7. Front.

At the second command the first three move straight to the front, dressing on the leading guide, who places himself on its left, the other threes oblique to the right till opposite their places in line, when each in succession marches forward.

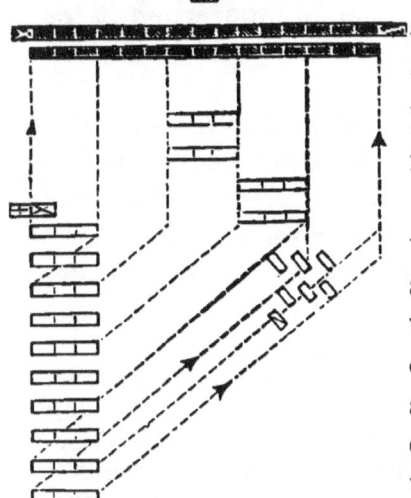

At the command *halt,* given when the leading three has advanced commandery distance, it halts, and at the sixth command given immediately after, dresses to the left. The other threes halt and dress to the left upon arriving in line. The rear ranks close to facing distance upon halting. The guide in rear places himself on the right of the front rank when the last three arrive in line.

If marching in double time, or *quick time* and the command is *double time,* the Commander orders: *guide left,* immediately after the command *march,* the leading three advance in quick time, the others oblique in double time; each resumes the forward march when opposite its place, taking the step and alignment from the guide (or dresses) as it arrives in line

If in double rank, and it is desired to form in single rank the command is, 1. *In single rank.* 2. *Right (or left) front into line,* etc. Each rear rank obliques until it has gained a distance equal to its front beyond the point where its front rank commenced the forward march, which is opposite its place in line when it too marches to the front, halting and dressing as explained.

If in single rank, to form in double rank in line, the principles are the same; the command will then be, 1. *In double rank.* 2. *Right front into line,* etc. The rear rank of each three obliques with and resumes the direct march at the same time as the front rank does, closing to facing distance on arriving in line.

To Face a Line to the Rear, and March it to the Rear.

1. *Threes right* (or *left*) *about.* 2. MARCH. 3 *Commandery.* 4. HALT. 5. *Left* (or *right*). 6. DRESS. 7. FRONT. Or, 3. *Guide* (*right* or *left*).

SCHOOL OF THE COMMANDERY.

The Commander passes between the nearest threes as they wheel about on fixed pivots, and places himself two yards in front of the center of the Commandery, and the guides wheel into their places.

From a halt to march a few paces to the rear:

1 *Commandery*. 2. ABOUT. 3. FACE. 4. *Forward*. 5. *Guide* (*right* or *left*). 6. MARCH. Or, if in march, 1. *To the rear*. 2. MARCH. 3. *Guide* (*right* or *left*).

The Guides and Standard Guard step into the rear rank, now become the front, unless the Secretary, Treasurer and Sentinel are formed with the Standard Guard and are in its front, which should so remain only temporarily. Having faced about, number one of each three now becomes number three, and the reverse.

To Break Threes to the Rear.

Marching in line, to pass obstacle.

1. (So many) *threes from right* (or *left*) *to rear*. 2. MARCH.

At the command *march* the designated three executes *left forward, threes left* on the three next on its left, which

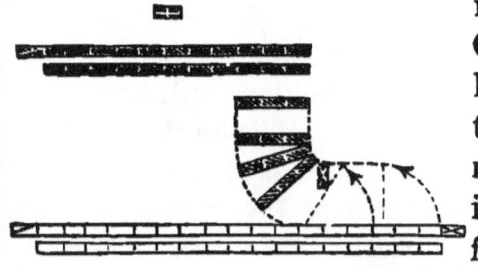

remains in line. The Commander points with his sword to the inner three which leads the movement. The guide, if the threes are broken from his side, closes in on the threes which remain in line; if from the opposite side, the guide on that flank follows in rear of the three next to him.

1. *Rear threes right* (or *left*) *front into line.* 2. *Double time.* 3. March.

The threes which were broken form in line, and the guide if on that side hastens to the point where the right of the Commandery will rest.

The Route Step.

Being in column of threes, marching.

1. *Route step.* 2. March.

At this command the swords are carried at will and the Knights need not preserve silence or keep the step, but each covers the file in front and maintains the regular distance.

Change of direction is affected by the same commands as when in the cadence step.

1. *Commandery.* 2. Attention.

At the second command the swords are brought to a *carry* and the cadence step is resumed.

To Form Column of Files from Column of Threes.

Being at a halt.

1. *Right* (or *left*) *by file.* 2. March.

At the first command the rear rank, if there be one, closes to facing distance.

At the second command the right file of the leading three of the front and rear rank moves forward, followed in succession by the files on his left. When the left file of the leading three is about to commence the oblique, the right file, front and rear rank of the second three move to the front, and so on to the rear of the column, keeping close to facing distance.

The guides (Vice-Commanders) precede and follow the leading and rear files.

If marching, the right file of the leading three continues the march, the others halt and resume the march at the proper time. The Commander places himself on the left of the leading guide.

To Form Column of Threes from Column of Files.

Being in march.

1 *Form threes.* 2. *Left* (or *right*) *oblique.* 3. MARCH.

At the command *march* the leading file of each three front and rear rank, if there be two ranks, moves forward two yards and halts, the rear rank Knights falling back to twenty-one inches; the other files oblique to the left and place themselves successively on the left of the leading files, the rear rank taking the distance of twenty one inches from the front rank; the other three successively form as explained for the first, the leading file of each three halting at twenty-one inches from the corresponding file of the next three in front. The leading guide places himself in front of the left file of the leading three.

To Form Column of Twos from Line, and Line from Column of Twos,

Is executed similar to like formations by threes.

To Form Column of Files from Line, and the Reverse.

In march the command is, 1. *By the right* (or *left*) *flank.* 2. MARCH. If the line is so formed add: 3. *Guide* (*right, left* or *center*).

From a halt, command: 1. *Right* (or *left*) 2. FACE. 3. *Forward.* 4 MARCH. If by facing the line is formed, add: 5. *Guide left* (*right* or *center*).

To Form Single Rank From Double Rank.

Being in line.

1. *Form single rank.* 2. *Three right* (or *left*). 3. MARCH.

All the threes wheel to the right at the command *march.* The front rank of the right threes, upon completion of the wheel, continues the march, and is conducted by the right guide who is in front of the file on the marching flank; the other ranks halt and successively resume the march when at fifty-four inches, wheeling distance, from the rank preceding.

The rearmost rank having its distance, the Commander orders:

1. *Threes left* (or *right*). 2. MARCH 3. *Commandery.* 4. HALT. 5. *Left* (or *right*). 6. DRESS. 7. FRONT. Or, 3. *Guide* (*right* or *left*).

Marching in Column to Form Single Rank.

1. *Form single Rank.* 2. MARCH.

At the second command, the front rank of the leading three continues the march, the others *halt* and resume the march when at wheeling distance, the rearmost three having its distance line, is formed as before.

If marching in *double time,* or in *quick time,* and the command be *double time,* the front rank of the leading three marches in double time; the others halt and take the double time when at wheeling distance.

The leading guide in column of threes at single rank distance places himself twenty-four inches in front of the file on the marching flank of the leading three. The rear guide follows at the same distance in rear of the file on the marching flank of the rear three.

In single rank the positions of the officers are the same as when in double rank. The Commandery executes all the movements explained for double rank, by similar commands and means.

For small Commanderies the single rank formation should generally be used.

To Form Double Rank.

Being in line single rank.

1. *Form double rank.* 2. *Threes right* (or *left*). 3. MARCH.

At the command *march*, the ranks of three wheel to the right, the leading rank halts the instant the wheel is completed; the others continue the march and halt successively upon closing to twenty-one inches from the rank preceding.

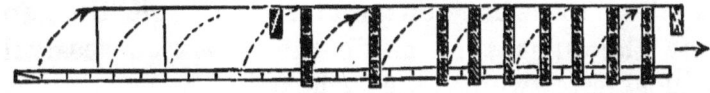

The rearmost rank having gained this distance, the Commander commands:

1. *Threes left* (or *right*). 2. MARCH. 3. *Commandery.* 4. HALT. 5 *Left* (or *right*). 6. DRESS. 7. FRONT. Or, 3 *Guide* (*right* or *left*)

The command is *threes left* (or *right*), according as the front ranks are on the right, or left, of their rear ranks. Should the original left three be in front, and its rear rank wanting, the front rank of the succeeding three instead of closing remains at its wheeling distance of fifty-four inches.

If the rearmost three is wanting in numbers to complete it, the Second Vice-Commander marches with it when the nature of his duties as guide, etc , does not render it impracticable; but when the Commandery is in line he is in the front rank on the left (or right).

Marching in column of threes, single rank distance, the front rank of each three being in front of its rear rank, *to form double ranks*, command :

1. *Form double rank.* 2. MARCH.

At the second command the leading rank halts; the others continue the march, each halting at twenty-one inches from the rank preceding, the rearmost rank having closed, the line is formed as before.

To Close to Double Rank Distance.

Being in march, threes at single rank distance,

1. *Double rank distance.* 2. *Double time.* 3. MARCH.

The leading rank continues in quick time; the other ranks close to twenty-one inches in double time and resume the quick time as do the others successively upon closing to twenty-one inches.

To Form Column of Divisions.

Being in line at a halt.

1. *Divisions right* (or *left*) *wheel.* 2. MARCH.

At the first command the First Vice-Commander as chief of the first division, and the Second Vice-Com-

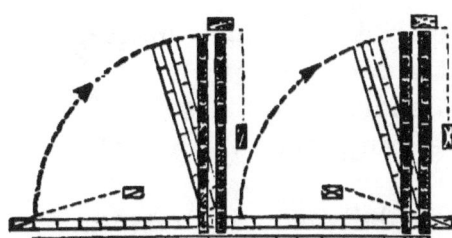

Double Rank without Standard.

mander, as chief of the second division, place themselves two yards in front of the center of and facing their divisions, repeat the command, *division right wheel.* At the second command, briskly repeated, each chief of division hastens by the shortest line to the point where the left of his division will rest and faces the late rear, the divisions wheel to the right on fixed pivots and the wheel of each division is conducted as explained in the wheelings of the Commandery, the

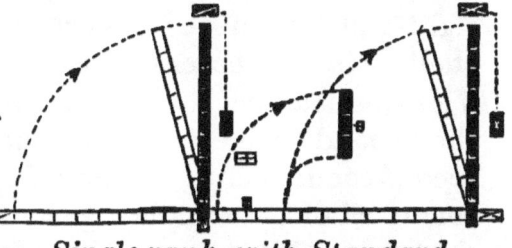

Single rank, with Standard.

Knights on the right and left of the divisions acting as right and left guides; when the division approaches the perpendicular its chief commands:

1. —— *Division.*   2. HALT   3. *Left*   4. DRESS   5. FRONT.

At the command *halt* the Knights on the left of the divisions place themselves so that their breasts will touch the right arms of their chiefs, who then step back two yards and each dresses his division and places himself in front of its center.

At the command *march, the Standard Guard* also wheels under direction of the Senior Aid, who is its chief, to the center of the column midway between the divisions.

If in march, the Commandery wheels into column by the same commands as at a halt. At the command *march* the pivots halt and mark time in their places, so as to conform to movement of the marching flank.

The position of the Commander is on the side of the guide, four yards from the flank and abreast of the leading division.

Whenever in column a subdivision is dressed, its chief places himself two yards in front of its center, except the chiefs of threes and sections who habitually remain on the flanks of their subdivisions.

1. *In three* (or *four*) *divisions.* 2. *Right wheel.* 3. MARCH.

The Commander having previously indicated the right and left of the divisions, so that the standard shall be in the center of the second division, the First Vice-Commander commands the leading division and the Second Vice-Commander the rear division. At the second command the Senior Aid steps to the front, takes command of the middle division, the Junior Aid takes the Senior Aid's place, and the left guide of this division quickly fills the interval at the left of the standard. If in two ranks the Junior Aid hastens to the right of the Standard Bearer, and the number *three*, who covered the Junior Aid, steps into the front rank on the left of the standard as soon as the interval is made.

The wheels are conducted as already explained; at the command *front* the chiefs of divisions place themselves in front of the centers of their divisions.

To Form Column of Divisions and Move Forward without Halting.

Being in line at a halt.

1. *Continue the march.* 2. *Divisions right* (or *left*) *wheel.* 3. MARCH. 4. *Forward.* 5. MARCH. 6. *Guide* (*right* or *left*).

The divisions wheel as before, except that the chiefs

of divisions remain in front of their centers. Each guide preserves his proper distance, and exactly covers the leading guide, who is careful to march straight and keep the correct step and cadence.

To put a Column of Divisions in Motion and Halt it.

1. *Forward.* 2. *Guide* (*right* or *left*). 3. MARCH, will put the column in motion from a halt; and 1. *Commandery.* 2. HALT, will halt it.

To Oblique.

The oblique is by the same commands and means, as heretofore explained, for obliquing in column of threes.

To Change Direction of a Column of Divisions.

Being in march.

1. *Column right* (or *left*). 2. MARCH.

At the first command the chief of the leading division commands, *right wheel;* at the command *march,* repeated by the chief, the division wheels to the right on a movable pivot; the chief adding 1. *Forward.* 2. MARCH, on the completion of the wheel; then adds *guide left* (or *right*), according to the position of the guide before the wheel.

The second division marches squarely up to the wheeling point and changes direction by the same means and commands from its chief.

The Standard Guard wheels on the same ground, under direcion of its chief (who does not leave his place on its right), and preserves its place in column.

When the right of a column is in front, the guide is *left,* and the reverse when the left is in front. This is not given as a rigid rule, but as a suggestion, the matter be'ng entirely at the discretion of the Commander.

In changing direction it is essential that the rear of the column should never be checked; each chief, therefore, whose place is in front of it, faces his division while wheeling, and sees that the guides take the full step of thirty, or thirty-five, inches, and the pivot nine, or eleven, inches, according to the time.

The guide in wheeling, is always on the marching flank without command; on its completion each chief of division, or double-section, cautions his subdivision *guide left,* or *right,* according as the guide was before the wheel.

Column Half Right or Left

Is similarly executed; each chief gives the preparatory command of *right* (or *left*) *half wheel.*

To put a Column of Divisions in March, and change direction at the same time.

1. *Forward.* 2. *Guide (right* or *left).* 3. *Column right* (or *left)*; or 3. *Column half right* (or *left).* 4. MARCH.

To Face a Column of Divisons to the Rear, and March it to the Rear.

1. *Threes right* (or *left) about.* 2. MARCH. 3. *Commandery.* 4. HALT; or 3 *Guide (left* or *right).*

At the fourth command, given the instant the threes complete the wheel, each chief goes to the left of his division and dresses it to the left, commands *front,* and places himself in front of its center.

SCHOOL OF THE COMMANDERY.

To march to the rear without halting, the Captain General announces the guide when the wheel is nearly completed.

If the column be faced to the rear and one division be smaller than the other, the guide of the second division regains the trace and wheeling distance on the march.

The Standard Guard conforms to these movements and carefully preserves its central position.

The leading division is always the *first division*, whether the right or left is in front.

To Form Line to the Left or Right from Column of Divisions.

Being at a halt.

1. *Left* (or *right*) *into line wheel.* 2. MARCH. 3. Commandery. 4. HALT. 5. *Right* (or *left*). 6 DRESS. 7. FRONT.

The first command is repeated by the Vice-Commanders, who promptly take their places on the left flanks of their divisions as guides, the one in the rear exactly covering the one in front.

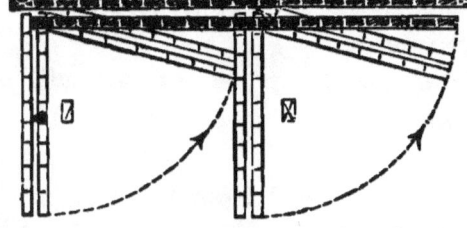

At the command *march* the Vice-Commanders turn their heads toward their divisions, repeat the command, and stand fast; the divisions wheel on a fixed pivot.

The Standard Guard wheels, conducted by and under direction of its chief, so that when the wheel is nearly completed he shall be opposite his place in line.

The Commander commands *halt*, and places himself in prolongation of the line marked by the Vice-Commanders where the marching flank of the leading divisions will rest, and faces the Vice Commanders.

At the sixth command, the divisions and Standard Guard dress up to the line; at the seventh command the Vice-Commanders take their places on the flanks of the Commandery.

If marching, the movement is executed as just explained, except at the command *march* the pivots halt and mark time in their places so as to conform to the movements of the marching flank.

To Form Line and Continue the March.

1. *Continue the march.* 2. *Left* (or *right*) *into line wheel.* 3. MARCH. 4. *Forward.* 5. MARCH. 6. *Guide left* (or *right*).

The chiefs repeat the commands to and including the third, and quickly return to their posts in line, so as to step off with the Commandery at the fifth command.

The pivots are careful to turn in their places as before, until the wheel is completed.

In long lines the guide may be *center*, when all will dress on the Standard Bearer.

To Form Line on the Right (or Left) from Column of Divisions.

Being in march.

The Commander indicates that the *guide* is *right* or

left, on the flank toward which the movement is to be executed and commands:

1. *On right* (or *left*) *into line.* 2. MARCH. 3. FRONT.

At the first command, the chief of the first division commands *right turn;* at the command *march*, repeated by its chief, the first division turns to the right, advances in the new direction, division distance, when the chief halts it, commands:
1. *Right.* 3. DRESS, and takes his place on its right. The Standard Guard and second division march straight forward, their chiefs successively command *right turn* in time to add MARCH when each is opposite its place in line; they are halted by the chiefs, the Standard Guard when at one and the division when at three yards from the line, who successively command *Right.* DRESS; and when the chief of the second division has given the second command, he takes his post on the left.

The Commander superintends the alignment from the right, and commands *front*.

A similar movement by threes from column of divisions or sections may be executed, as before explained; each three in succession breaking from its division by wheeling when opposite its place in line; the command, when in columns of sections or divisions, being preceded by, 1. **By** *threes.* 2. *On right into line,* etc.

SCHOOL OF THE COMMANDERY.

To Break into Divisions.

From a halt.

1. *Right* (or *left*) *by divisions.* 2. MARCH. 3. *Guide left* (or *right*).

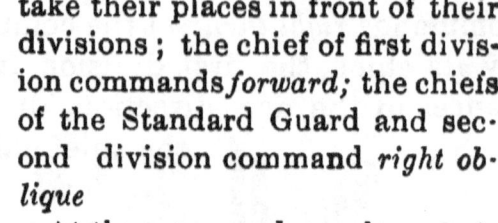

At the first command, the Vice-Commanders quickly take their places in front of their divisions; the chief of first division commands *forward;* the chiefs of the Standard Guard and second division command *right oblique*

At the command *march* repeated by the chief of the right division, the division moves forward, the chief repeating *guide left.* The chiefs of the Standard Guard and left division successively command *march* the instant they are severally disengaged

The Senior Aid commands *forward* and adds MARCH the instant the Standard Guard is opposite the center of the first division, and so regulates the steps, that it may immediately gain and preserve its proper distance.

The chief of the left division commands, 1. *Forward,* and adds 2. MARCH. 3. *Guide left,* the instant the Knight on its left arrives in trace of the guide of the leading division; the guide is careful to regulate his steps so as to preserve the proper distance.

If marching, the chief of the first division repeats the command, indicating the place of the guide.

The chiefs of Standard Guard and second division command, 1. *Standard Guard* (or *Second division*). 2.

Mark time, repeat the command *march*, adding *right oblique* in time to command *march* the instant they are disengaged; the movement is completed as from a halt.

To Re-form the Commandery.

Being at a halt.

1. *Form Commandery.* 2. *Left* (or *right*) *oblique.* 3 MARCH. 4. FRONT.

At the second command the chief of the first division commands, 1. *Forward.* 2. *Guide right.* The chiefs of the Standard Guard and second division command *left oblique.*

At the command *march,* repeated by the chiefs, the first division advances division distance, when its chief commands, 1. *First Division.* 2. HALT. 3. *Right.* 4. DRESS, and returns to his place on the right flank.

The Standard Guard obliques to the left, its chief commanding 1. *Forward* in time to add 2. MARCH 3. *Guide right* the instant the guard is opposite its place in line. When in rear of the line its chief halts it and commands, 1. *Right.* 2. DRESS.

The second division marches to its place in line by the same commands and means as described for the Standard Guard, is halted at three yards from the line, and its chief commands, 1. *Right.* 2. DRESS, and takes his post on its left.

The Commander superintends the alignment from the right, and gives the fourth command.

If *marching* in *quick time*, and the command be *double time*, the Commander commands *Guide right* (or *left*) immediately after the command *march*, the chief of the leading division commands *Forward*, MARCH, and repeats the indication for the guide. The chiefs of the Standard Guard and second division repeat the commands *double time, march,* and when they are about to arrive in line, command *quick time,* adding MARCH the instant they are abreast of the leading division The divisions and Standard Guard united, the Vice Commanders return to their posts on the flanks.

If marching in *double time* the chief of the first division, at the first command of the Commander, commands *quick time,* repeats the command *march,* and also the command for the guide.

To March a Column of Divisions by the Flank and Re-form the Column.

Being at a halt.

1. *Right* (or *left*). 2. FACE. 3. *Forward.* 4. MARCH. 5. *Guide left* (or *right*).

The Vice Commanders place themselves in front of the leading files, and the Standard Guard marches in column of files in the center between the divisions. The Commander is on the side of the guide, four yards from the flank, abreast of the chiefs of division, or on a line midway between them.

If in march the divisions may be moved to the right or left by the commands, 1. *By the right* (or *left*) *flank.* 2. MARCH. 3. *Guide left* (or *right*).

Or, *if at a halt, or in march,* by the command:

1. *Threes right* (or *left*). 2. MARCH. 3. *Guide left* (or *right*).

The Vice Commanders quickly place themselves in front of their divisions, as in column of threes; the

SCHOOL OF THE COMMANDERY.

Standard Guard wheels as other threes do, and maintains its central position.

To Form in Column Again.

If the divisions are marching by the flank in columns of files, command, 1. *By the left* (or *right*) *flank*. 2. MARCH. 3. *Guide left* (or *right*).

If marching in columns of threes, as explained, the Commander commands:

1. *Threes left* (or *right*). 2. MARCH. 3. *Guide left* (or *right*), or 3. *Commandery*. 4. HALT.

The threes and Standard Guard wheel to the left into column of divisions; the Vice-Commanders take their positions and exact distances are carefully preserved.

If halted, the chiefs dress their commands and promptly take their places in front of the centers of their division.

To Advance by the Right or Left of Divisions from Line.

1. *Divisions*. 2. *Right* (or *left*) *forward*. 3. *Threes right* (or *left*). 4. MARCH. 5. *Guide right* (or *left*).

At the second command the Vice-Commanders quickly place themselves in front of the centers of their divisions. At the command *march* each division executes the movement from its right. The chiefs place themselves in

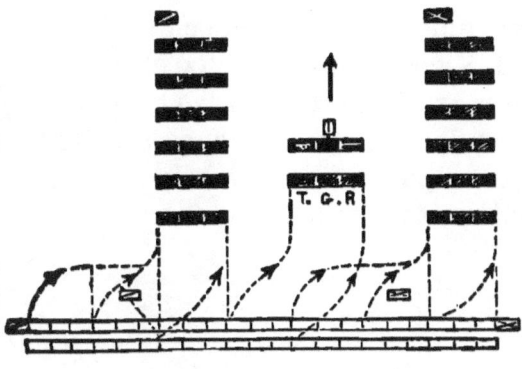

front of the left files of the leading threes, the Commander is midway between and on a line with the Vice-Commanders.

The Standard Guard wheels to the right, and follows the division whose rear file is next to it, until it is opposite the center between the divisions when it wheels to the left and marches into its place in the center, under direction of its chief.

To Form in Line again.

1. *Divisions.* 2. *Left* (or *right*) *front into line.* 3. MARCH. 4. *Commandery.* 5 HALT. 6. *Right* (or *left*). 7. DRESS. 8. FRONT.

The Vice-Commanders hasten to their posts on the flanks.

The Standard Guard obliques to the left, halts in rear of its place in line, under direction of its chief, and dresses to the right. The command *halt* is given when the leading threes have advanced division distance.

To Form Column of Threes from Column of Divisions.

1. *Divisions.* 2. *Right* (or *left*) *forward.* 3. *Threes, right* (or *left*). 4. MARCH.

The First Vice-Commander takes his place in column of threes; The Second Vice-Commander faces about and takes his place in rear of the column, as his division passes; and the Standard Guard marches straight forward, wheeling to the right into its place in rear of the division in its front as it passes.

SCHOOL OF THE COMMANDERY. 85

To Form Column of Divisions From Column of Threes.

1. *Divisions.* 2. *Left (or right) front into line.* 3. MARCH.
4 *Commandery.* 5 HALT.

At the second command the Vice Commanders place themselves on the left and opposite the centers of their divisions.

At the third command each division executes left front into line; the chiefs place themselves in front of the centers of their divisions; the Standard Guard obliques to the left and marches to the center between the divisions, under direction of its chief. The command *halt* is given when the leading division has advanced division distance; each chief dresses his division to the right, and takes his place in front of its center.

If executed in double time, or in quick time, and the command be *double time,* the Commander commands: *Guide right* (or *left*) immediately after the command *march.*

The Display Drill.

REMARKS.—Thus far the movements have been chiefly legitimate or in accord with the U. S. Infantry Tactics, substituting *threes* for *fours*, *divisions* for *platoons*, dispensing with *file closers*, causing the Vice-Commanders to perform the double duty of lieutenants and sergeants, and providing for a Standard Guard.

The movements which follow are in harmony with the principles laid down

As it not desirable to describe minutely every detail that may arise in the movements of a Commandery the Commander will use his discretion in supplying any detail or omission. His decision should be final in any case not supplied by the tactics.

The Standard Bearer (Guard) may carry the standard, dispensing with the Aides, but his movements will be similar to those of the full guard. If the Standard Bearer does not carry the standard the Knights composing the Standard Guard should fall in as other Knights.

To Form Column of Threes by a Flank Movement from Column of Files.

Being in march.

1. *Left* (or *right*) *flank by threes.* 2. MARCH.

At the first command the First Vice-Commander

places himself twelve inches to the left of number three of the leading three, faced in the direction toward which the column is marching. At the command *march* both the First Vice Commander and the leading three march by the left flank; the others move forward until each three in succession has gained the ground from which the first three marched by the flank, when it executes the same movement, follows in trace of the three next in its front, and maintains its proper distance in the column The Second Vice-Commander turns to the left, so as to follow the left file of the rear three.

To Form Line Faced to the Rear from Column of Threes

1. *Right* (or *left*) *front into line, faced to rear.* 2. MARCH. 3. *Commandery.* 4. HALT. 5. *Right* (or *left*). 6. DRESS. 7. FRONT.

The movement is executed as previously explained for *right front into line*, except that at the command *halt* the leading three wheels *left about* on a fixed pivot and dresses toward the point of rest; the other threes successively wheel about on the same line and dress as before explained

A similar movement may be made from column of sections, except that the sections do not halt until three yards beyond the line; the sections are then wheeled, threes left about by the chiefs, who successively command *right dress;* the Commander verifies the alignment, and commands *front.*

This will reverse the order of threes, but the following consecutive movements will place them in their original position in column of sections:

Form column of threes, by the commands *threes right* or, *right forward threes right,* etc., then *form sections right oblique,* hereafter explained (page 92).

To Form Line by two Movements from Column of Threes.

A part of the column having changed direction to the right, to form line to the left:

1. *Threes left.* 2. *Rear threes left front into line.* 3. MARCH. 4 FRONT.

Those threes which have changed direction execute *threes left,* halt and dress to the right, at the command of the chief of the leading division, the rear threes execute *left front into line,* and dress upon the established line at command of the chief of the rear division; at the completion of the movement the Commander commands *front.*

To Form Line Faced to the Rear, by two Movements.

A part of the column of threes, having changed direction to the right as before:

1. *Threes right.* 2. *Rear threes left front into line, faced to rear.* 3. MARCH.

The threes which have changed direction wheel to the right, halt and dress to the left at the command of the chief of the leading division, the rear threes execute *left front into line, faced to rear*, obliquing far enough to the left of their places in line that in wheeling (to the right) about they shall come squarely up to their proper positions and dress on the new alignment.

At the completion of the movement the Commander commands *front*.

If the column has changed direction to the left, the line is formed to the right by inverse commands, thus:

1. *Threes left.* 2. *Rear threes right front into line*, etc.

To Change Front.

Being in line.

1. *Change front on right* (or *left*) *three.* 2. *Threes right* (or *left*). 3. MARCH. 4. *Commandery.* 5. HALT. 6. *Right.* 7. DRESS. 8. FRONT.

At the third command the threes wheel to the right; the First Vice-Commander quickly places himself on the right of the first three and, with it, moves straight to the front; the others oblique to the left and successively march to the front when opposite their places in line. The command *halt* is given when the leading three has advanced commandery distance, and the movement is completed as in *left front into line*.

1. *Change front forward on right* (or *left*) *three.* 2. *Threes right* (or *left*). 3. MARCH. 4. *Commandery.* 5. HALT. 6. *Right.* 7. DRESS. 8. FRONT.

At the command *march*, the threes wheel to the right;

the first three advances a distance equal to its front
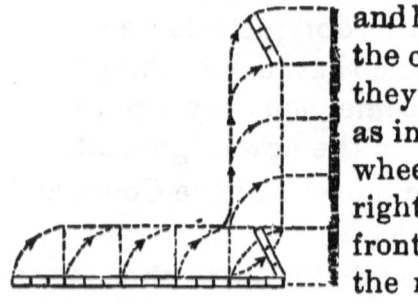
and halts at the fifth command; the other threes advance until they execute the same moment as in *right forward, threes right*, wheeling to the left as if the right three had marched to the front instead of wheeling to the right, and the movement is then completed as in *on right into line.*

To Form Line on the Standard Guard from Column of Threes.

1. *On Standard into line.* 2. *Threes right about* Rear threes, *left front into line.* 4. MARCH. 5. FRONT.

At the fourth command the threes in front of the standard wheel to the right about, and execute *left*
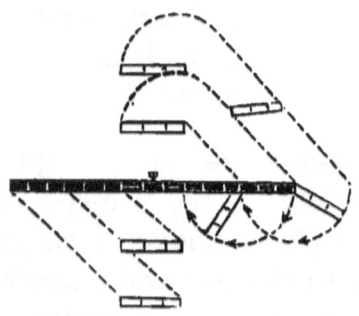
front into line faced to rear, obliquing to the left of their places in line a distance equal to their front, so that in wheeling about, after passing the new line, they shall be opposite their places and not lap over on the Standard Guard.

The rear threes execute *left front into line* as before explained. *If in march,* the Senior Aide at the fourth command, orders his guard to halt. Dress on the center.

To Form and Wheel in Line from Column of Threes.
1. *Threes left* (or *right*). 2. *Left* (or *right*) *wheel.* 3. MARCH. 4. *Commandery.* 5. HALT. 6. *Right* (or *left*). 7 DRESS. 8. FRONT.

The threes wheel to the left; and the instant they

are united in line the Commandery wheels to the left on a movable pivot, as before explained, and is halted, or marched forward by the usual commands and me ns.

To Form Column of Sections from Line.

Being at a halt.

1. *Sections right* (or *left*) *wheel.* 2. MARCH. 3. *Commandery.* 4. HALT. 5. *Left* (or *right*). 6. DRESS. 7. FRONT.

At the first command the First Vice-Commander moves to a place about forty four inches in front of the point at which the left file of the leading section will rest, and faces to the left (rear of column); the Second Vice-Commander marches straight forward, halts and faces to the right, on the prolongation of a line upon which the left files of each section will rest when the wheel is completed; the Vice-Commanders are now facing each other At the second command each section wheels on a fixed pivot; the Standard Guard wheels to the center of the column between the sections which were on its right and left before the movement commenced.

At the command *halt*, given as the sections approach the quarter circle, the left files step promptly up to the place where the left of their sections will rest and on a line between the Vice-Commander, facing the First Vice-Commander, each opposite the chief of his section, perpendicular to its former position; the Vice-Commanders see that the guides cover each other; the chiefs of sections, without moving out of their places, superintend the alignment of their sections, the commands being given by the Commander.

At the seventh command the First Vice-Commander in front faces about and the Vice-Commander in rear closes up to forty-four inches from the left file of the rearmost section.

If marching: At the second command the Vice-Commanders hasten to their places in column; the pivots halt, mark time in their places, and conform to the movements of the marching flank. Chiefs of sections from their places on the right, without turning the head, see that in all movements their sections keep dressed and preserve the proper step and distance, the cautions being given in a low tone of voice and only when necessary.

To Wheel into Column of Sections from Line and Advance without Halting.

1. *Continue the march.* 2. *Sections right* (or *left*) *wheel.* 3. MARCH 4 *Forward.* 5. MARCH. 6. *Guide left* (or *right*).

The sections wheel as before except that the Vice-Commanders hasten to their posts in the column and the Commander gives the fourth command in time to add *march* the instant the sections arrive at the perpendicular from the former front.

To Form Column of Sections from Column of Threes.

Being in march.

1. *Form sections.* 2. *Left* (or *right*) *oblique.* 3 MARCH. 4. *Guide left* (or *right*).

At the third command the odd threes take a short step and *mark time;* the even threes oblique to the left until opposite their places in section, when they resume the *forward*. The Commander gives the fourth command the instant the threes are united in sections, and all take the full step.

If the threes are reversed, that is, when the odd become the even threes in the column of threes, sections are formed upon the same principles but to the right. The command being, 1. *Form sections*. 2. *Right oblique*, etc. Or, 1. *By section*. 2. *Threes right*. 3. MARCH, explained below.

To Form Column of Sections to the Left or Right, from Column of Threes.

Being in column of threes marching:

1. *By section.* 2. *Threes left* (or *right*). 3. MARCH. 4 *Guide left* (or *right*).

At the second command the First Vice-Commander places himself on the left of the second three.

At the command *march* the First Vice-Commander advances and wheels in front of the file on his right; the leading and second three wheel to the left on movable pivots, uniting in section on the completion of the wheel

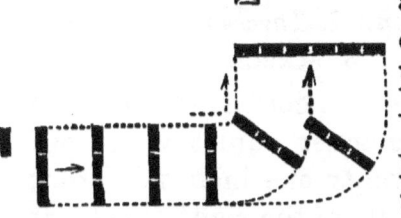

and marching perpendicular to their former direction. The other threes advance and, by section, execute the same movement on the same ground, the Standard Guard advances and wheels to the left in rear of the center of the section in its front. The Second Vice-Commander shortens his steps as the rear threes wheel and follows in the column of sections as explained before.

To Break into Column of Threes from Column of Sections.

1. *Right by threes.* 2. MARCH. 3. *Guide left* (or *right*).

At the command *march*, the right threes move straight forward; the left threes as soon as disengaged, oblique to the right into column of threes; the Vice-Commanders and Standard Guard also obliquing to their places. The obliquing threes resume the forward march, without command, as soon as they gain their places in the column, and steps are regulated accordingly.

To halt after the formation of the column, the Commander immediately after *march* commands *Commandery*, and adds *halt* the instant the left files of the obliquing threes have gained the rear of the left files of the threes in their front. The column halts and those that obliqued face to the front.

To Form Columns of Threes to the Right or Left, from Column of Sections.

Being in march.

1. *By section.* 2. *Threes right* (or *left*). 3. MARCH.

At the second command the First Vice Commander quickly places himself twenty-one inches in front of the left file of the right three; at the command *march* he wheels to the right as if he were the marching flank of a rank of three leading the column; the threes of the leading section execute *threes right,* following the trace of the First Vice Commander, the rear sections march forward, and each in succession executes the

THE DISPLAY DRILL. 95

same movement from the same ground   The Standard Guard wheels on the same ground to its place in the column; the Second Vice-Commander closes to his place twenty-one inches from the left file of the three in rear.

To March in Line.

Before the movement by threes from column of section is completed, command:

1. *Threes left.* 2 *Rear section forward*, and add 3. MARCH, the instant the rearmost section is about to wheel by threes; the threes that have changed direction execute *threes left;* the rear section marches straight forward, and as the line is formed, the Commander commands, *guide right* (or *left*). The Standard Guard wheels as a rank of three.

If the column be a long one the line may be formed thus:

1. *Threes left.* 2. *Rear sections left front into line.* 3. *Double time.* 4 MARCH. 5. *Guide right.* Or, 5. *Commandery.* 6. HALT. 7. *Right.* 8. DRESS. 9. FRONT.

And the movement is executed upon the principles before explained; the sixth command being given when the right threes have advanced commandery distance.

To Form Columns of Threes from Column of Sections, and March to the Rear.

1. *Threes right and left about.* 2. MARCH. 3. *Guide center.*

At the second command the right threes execute the *right about*, and the left threes the *left about*, on fixed pivots, the Standard Guard executes the movement *to the rear, march*, and regulates its steps so as to maintain its place; the First Vice-Commander turns to the right, and places himself directly in rear (after the about) of the Standard Bearer, advancing quickly until he is abreast of and between the rearmost threes. The Second Vice-Commander also turns to the right and places himself on a line with the First Vice-Commander and Standard Bearer, and abreast of and between the leading threes. The Commander marches two yards in front of the Second Vice Commander. The threes of each section carefully preserve section distance and the alignment with each other.

1. *Form sections.* 2. *Threes right and left about.* 3. MARCH. 4. *Guide left.*

At the command *march* the threes wheel about on fixed pivots, reuniting the sections, the Standard Guard executing *to the rear, march* as before, the Vice Commanders resume their places, and the guide is then announced. Or,

1. *By threes.* 2. *Front to rear.* 3. MARCH. 4. *Guide center.*

Being in column of sections marching.

At the third command the threes of the leading section wheel from the center *right and left about* into columns of threes, the pivots describing circles whose radii are twelve inches; the others advance and the threes of each section in succession execute the same movement on the same ground.

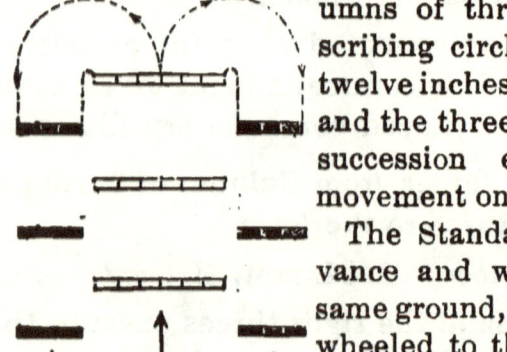

The Standard Guard will advance and wheel about, on the same ground, into the column that wheeled to the right; the Vice-Commanders place themselves twenty one inches in front of the left files of the leading threes, the First Vice-Commander in advance of the column that wheeled to the right about, and the Second Vice-Commander taking his place in lead of the other column as it passes. The Commander marches between and on a line with the Vice-Commanders at the head of the column.

1. *Form sections.* 2. *Front to rear.* 3. MARCH.

This is given after the columns of threes are formed as just explained, as soon as the heads of the column have passed the rearmost section, or may be deferred for a short distance. At the third command the leading threes wheel about toward the center, unite in section and march toward their former rear; the others in succession execute the same movement on the same ground, following in column of sections; the officers resume their places, and the Standard Guard, after wheeling, obliques to its place in the center.

To Close Sections to Half Distance or in Mass.

Being in column.

1. *To half* (or such) *distance close column.* 2. MARCH.

At the command *march* the leading section stands fast, if at a halt, or halts if in march, at the caution of its chief; the others advance and successively halt at the given distance and are promptly dressed at command of the chiefs of the sections.

If in line, command:

1. *To half* (or such) *distance close column.* 2. *Sections right* (or *left*) *wheel.* 3 MARCH.

At the third command the sections wheel to the right and the leading section is halted and dressed by its chief; the others advance, on completing the wheel, and the movement is completed as before explained

These movements may be executed in double time; when the leading section takes up and continues the march in quick time on completion of the wheel; the others close to the designated distance and successively take the step and cadence, from the guide in their front at the command *quick time*, MARCH, by the chief of their section.

To take Wheeling Distance from Column of Sections in Mass, etc.

1. *Take wheeling distance.* 2. MARCH.

At the second command the leading section marches forward, at the caution of its chief; the others halt, if in march, or stand fast if at a halt, and successively take up the march, at the commands of their chiefs, when the designated distance is gained.

To Form Column of Sections, Forward, from Line.

1. *Center forward.* 2. *Threes left and right.* 3. MARCH. 4 *Guide left* (or *right*).

At the second command the First Vice-Commander places himself in front of the left file of the center section. At the command *march* the center section and First Vice-Commander move straight forward; the threes of the right wing execute *left forward threes left*, and those of the left wing execute *right forward threes right;* the Second Vice-Commander follows the column of threes on the left, falling back to his place in column of sections, as the rear threes unite in section.

If the Standard Guard is present the First Vice-Commander places himself in front of the Junior Aide and the Standard Guard and First Vice-Commander lead the movement

Column of sections is thus formed when the original right is the center of the line.

To Form Line to the Front, from Column of Sections.

1. *Right and left front into line.* 2. MARCH. 3. *Commandery.* 4. HALT. 5. *Center.* 6. DRESS. 7. FRONT.

At the command *march* the Standard Guard (or center section) marches straight to the front; the right threes execute *right front into line*, and the left threes execute *left front into line*.

Line is formed in this way from column of sections when the original center of the Commandery is at the head of the column, and may be executed in double time as before explained

To Form Line by Two Movements, from Column of Sections at Half Distance.

1. *Threes right* (or *left*). 2. *Left* (or *right*) *threes on right* (or *left*) *into line*. 3. MARCH. 4. FRONT.

At the command *march* the right threes execute *threes right*, move forward commandery distance and the First Vice Commander commands, 1. *Right wing* 2. HALT. 3. *Right.* 4. DRESS and takes his place on the right. The left threes execute *on right into line*, the Second Vice Commander quickly placing himself in front of the leading three commands, 1. *Left wing.* 2. HALT. 3. *Right* 4 DRESS, giving the second command as the leading three of the left wing arrives in rear of the line and places himself on the left, in prolongation of the line facing to the right On the completion of the movement the Commander commands *front*, and the Second Vice Commander takes his place on the left flank.

If the Standard Guard is present the right threes wheel to the right as before; when the wheel is completed the right threes that were in the rear of the guard immediately oblique to the left by lengthened steps; the First Vice Commander passes by their front to the right and commands *forward*, adding MARCH the instant that those who are obliquing have united in line with the other right threes; gives the command before explained, and places himself on the right The Standard Guard and left threes march forward as before; the leading three advances nearly two yards beyond the left of the right threes and wheels to the right on a moveable pivot, leaving room between it and the right wing for the Standard Guard, which wheels to the right when opposite its place in line; the other left threes successively wheel to the right when opposite their places in line, and the movement is completed as before explained.

The movement may be executed without halting, thus:

1. *Threes right* (or *left*). 2. *Left* (or *right*) *threes on right* (or *left*) *into line*. 3. *Double time* 4 MARCH. 5 *Guide right* (or *left*)

The left threes and Standard Guard execute the movement as before explained, but in double time, taking the step and alignment from the right wing, as they successively arrive on the line. The Commander commands *guide right* when the right threes have united in line, they then advance in quick time

THE DISPLAY DRILL.

To Form Line by Three Movements from Column of Sections.

1. *By section.* 2. *Threes right and left.* 3. MARCH.

Being in column of sections at half distance. At the command *march* the left three of the leading section wheels to the left and the right three wheels to the right, marching in opposite directions; the other sections advance and, except the one in the rear, successively execute the same movements from the same ground. The First Vice-Commander is in lead of the right threes, and the Second Vice Commander quickly places himself in lead of the left threes as before explained when the movement is commenced. [If the Standard Guard is in the column it does not wheel but marches straight to the front and *marks time* on a line with the marching flanks of the threes that wheeled into columns, right and left] The threes regulate their steps to preserve wheeling distance. When the rearmost section approaches the point from which other sections broke into threes, command:

1 *Form line.* 2. *Threes left and right.* 3 MARCH.
4. *Guide center.*

At the second command the chief of the section that has not broken cautions it to *forward*, and at the command *march,* given the instant the rear section has

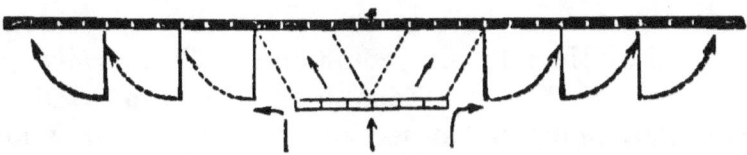

gained the ground from which the others wheeled by threes, this section marches straight forward; the threes on its left wheel to the right, those on the right wheel to the left into line, the Commander announces the guide and places himself two yards in front of the Commandery.

[If the Standard Guard is present the command *march* is given, so that the rearmost section may break and its threes oblique to the right and left of the Standard Guard]

Column of sections may then be formed thus: 1. *Center forward* 2. *Threes left and right.* 3 MARCH. as before explained.

[If the Standard Guard is in line, and it is desired to cause it to occupy its central place in column, the command will be 1. *Center forward.* 2 *Threes left and right.* 3. *Standard Guard, post.* 4 MARCH. 5 *Guide left* (or *right*). At the command *march* the movement is executed as before, except that the Standard Guard steps backward to unmask the approaching columns; the threes of the leading section oblique toward the center until united in section, then march forward. The Standard Guard marks time and resumes the *forward march* as soon as the threes of the section originally in its front unite.]

The column is now left in front with the original left threes still on its left, the First Vice-Commander in advance. To cause the threes to occupy their original position in column of sections right in front repeat the commands for the formation of line by three movements, and the formation of column of sections on the center forward, as before; or consecutive movements indicated by the following commands: *Threes right* (or *left*) *about.* 2. MARCH. Each three wheels on a fixed pivot and, reuniting in section, the column marches

THE DISPLAY DRILL. 103

to the late rear, then: 1. *By section.* 2. *Threes left.* 3. MARCH. (*Vide* page 94.)

To Form Column of Twos, from Column of Sections.
1. *Center forward.* 2. *Files left and right* 3. MARCH.

At the command *march* the right threes execute *left forward files left*, and the left threes execute *right forward files right;* the standard bearer marches forward and the Senior Aide and Junior Aide form a rank of two in his rear, all maintaining the same distances. It now being a column of files, double rank, the leading files shorten the steps until the Commander seeing that the rear files have closed to their places, commands *forward, march*, when all take the thirty inch step.

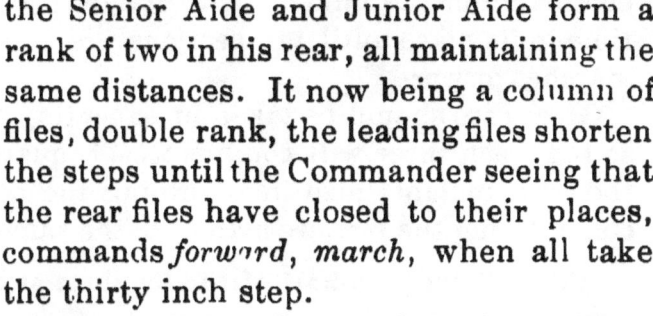

To form into column of sections again, command:
1. *Right and left front into sections.*
2. MARCH.

The right files of each section execute *right front into line*, and the left files of each section execute *left front into line*, thus reforming each section; the rear sections shorten the step until each in succession has gained its proper distance The standard-bearer shortens his step and the Senior Aide and Junior Aide take their places on his right and left.

Similar movemen's from the center of double sections may be made by similar commands and means.

To Wheel in Circles for Display.
From column of sections.
1. *Threes in circle right and left wheel* 2 MARCH.
3. *Guide left* (or *right*).

At the command *march* the First Vice Commander

takes two steps to the front and halts; the Second Vice-Commander steps backward the same distance and halts; the right threes wheel on fixed pivots to the right, numbers one marking time, and conforming to the movement of the marching flank; the left threes wheel to the left in like manner on numbers three. When the circles (full about) are completed and the sections re-formed, the column moves forward at the command for the guide. The Standard Guard marks time in its place until the sections are reformed, then marches forward.

Great care should be taken in executing the wheels, so that each three will complete each quarter circle at the same instant; also in reforming the sections and commencing the *forward march*, at the same instant.

To Wheel One-half of the Sections at a Time.

Being in march.

1. *Right threes in circle right wheel.* 2. MARCH.

At the command *march* the right threes wheel as just described, and when completed march forward as before; the Standard Guard by *right side steps* places itself in rear of the wheeling threes and marks time until the full about is completed, then follows the three in its front. When the wheel is nearly completed the Commander commands, 1. *Left threes in circle left wheel*, and adds, 2. MARCH, so that the left threes will commence the wheel the instant the right threes resume the *forward march* When the left threes complete the wheel the sections will be reunited, if the movement is executed properly; the column moves forward without command and the **Standard Guard** obliques to the left into its place.

THE DISPLAY DRILL. 105

Similar movements may be executed when marching in line, and by the similar commands and means.

To Advance Even Sections to the Front of Odd Sections in Column.

1. *Threes in circle right and left wheel.* **2.** *Even sections forward.* **3.** MARCH.

At the command *march* the right threes of the first, third and other odd sections wheel in circles full about to the right, and the left threes of the same sections wheel in circles to the left, on movable pivots, each pivot Knight describing a circle whose radius is twelve inches; the second, fourth, and other even sections march straight forward, passing between the threes of the section in their front as they complete the half circle. The First Vice-Commander shortens his steps and moves forward; the Second Vice Commander follows the rear section, if it be an even section, and halts when he has gained the distance of two yards from the section that is wheeling by threes; when the movement is completed he closes to fifty-four inches from the left file of the rear section and follows the column; if the rear be an odd section, he takes two backward steps and halts as before. When the wheeling threes have completed their circles and reunite in sections, they march forward and are careful to regain the proper, section, distance if lost.

To move the former odd, now the even, sections forward into their original places in column, the commands and movements are exactly similar to those just explained.

[If the Standard Guard is in the column it advances

between the wheeling threes; the sections regulating the steps so as to maintain their position. The Commander commands, 1. *To the rear.* 2. MARCH, repeats the movement just explained, and again executes *to the rear march*, which brings the standard to its original position].

To Deploy Column of Sections

Being at a halt.

1. *On first section deploy column.* 2 *Left.* 3. FACE. 4. *Forward* 5. MARCH 6. FRONT.

At the first command the First Vice-Commander faces about and places himself on the right of the first section, whose chief commands, *stand fast*, and immediately dresses it to the right. The other sections face to the left at the third command.

At the command *march* the Standard Guard and all the sections, except the first, being faced to the left, march straight forward; the chief of the second section commands, 1. *By the right flank*, and adds, 2. MARCH. 3. *Guide right* the instant he is opposite his place in line. This section halts in rear of the line at command of its chief who immediately adds, 1. *Right.* 2. DRESS.

The Guides of the rear sections march abreast of each other and parallel to the second; each chief in succession marching his section *by the right flank*, and dressing it upon the line as described for the second section. The Second Vice Commander hastens to the point where the left of the line will rest; the Commander superintends the alignment and commands *front.*

If *marching*, command, 1. *On first section deploy column.* 2. *By the left flank.* 3. MARCH. At the third command the first section is halted and dressed by its chief; the rear sections and guard march by the left flank and the movement is completed as before.

1. *On rear section deploy column.* 2. *Right.* 3. FACE. 4. *Forward.* 5. MARCH 6. FRONT.

Being at a halt   Four sections are supposed to be in the column.

At the first command the First Vice Commander faces and marches to the right, halts and faces about in front of the chief of the first section; the Second Vice Commander hastens to place himself in the place vacated by the First Vice-Commander and faces him; the chief of the fourth section commands, *Fourth section stand fast*

At the command *fce* the other sections face to the right. At the fifth command the rear section marches straight forward, halts one yard from the First Vice-Commander and its chief dresses it upon the Vice-Commander; the First Vice-Commander faces about, marches in prolongation of the line, halts where the right of the Commandery will rest, and again faces about exactly in front of the Second Vice-Commander facing him. In the meantime the other sections move forward, at the fifth command, led by their chiefs, at section distance, parallel with each other; the guide of the third section commands, 1. *Third section.* 2 *By the left flank,* and adds, 3. MARCH. 4. *Guide left* the instant the fourth section is unmasked. When within one yard from the established line its chief halts it and immediately commands, 1. *Third section.* 2. *Left.* 3. DRESS, when it dresses upon the line.

When the guide of the third section commands *by the left flank, march,* the second section advances section distance and then marches by the left flank in the same manner, and is dressed as described for the third section, and so on with the remaining section.

The Commander commands *front* when the movement is completed, and the Vice-Commanders take their places in line.

If marching the commands would be, 1. *On rear section deploy column.* 2. *By the right flank.* 3. MARCH. 4. FRONT.

The fourth section continues to march straight forward at the caution of its chief; the others march *by the right flank*, and the movement is completed as before,

It is of great importance in all deployments that commands be promptly given and distances accurately maintained.

1. *On* (such a) *section* (or Standard Guard) *deploy column.* 2. *Right and left.* 3. FACE. 4. *Forward.* 5 MARCH. 6. FRONT.

Being at a halt

At the command *march* the sections in front of the designated section deploy to the right; those in rear deploy to the left. The designated section, as soon as unmasked, is marched forward at command of its chief to the line established by the Vice-Commanders, as before described, and is dressed to the right against the Vice-Commanders, who then face about and march in prolongation of the line, halt where the right and left of the line will rest, and each faces toward the other. The other sections are dressed toward the designated section, and the movement is completed upon principles before explained.

THE DISPLAY DRILL. 109

If in march the designated section is halted in rear of the line; the sections in front of the designated section are marched *by the right flank;* those in rear are marched *by the left flank*, and the movement is completed as before.

To Form Double Sections from Column of Sections.

Remarks.—The first and second sections form the first double section; the third and fourth sections form the second double-section, and so on.

The First Vice-Commander is chief of the leading double-section, the Second Vice-Commander chief of the one in rear. If there are three double-sections the Senior Aide takes command of the second. If there are four double-sections the standard occupies the center of the second and the Senior Aide commands it, the Junior Aide commands the third. If more than four the Senior Aide commands the center double-section having the standard; the Junior Aide commands the one in its rear. The Knight on the right acts as chief of double-section unprovided for. When double sections are dissolved the chiefs resume their places. The Standard Guard may retain its identity and march between the double-sections that were on its right and left, if desired; or it may form the left three of a section, in which event it will execute the movement with its section. Or the standard bearer alone may march as if the full guard was with him. These various positions are determined by the number of Knights in line.

Being at a halt the Commander commands:

1. *Form double-sections.* 2. *Left oblique.* 3. MARCH.

At the second command the chiefs of the odd numbered sections command, 1. *Forward.* 2. *Guide right,* and the chiefs of the even numbered sections command, *left oblique*. At the command *march*, repeated by the chiefs, the odd sections advance section distance, their chiefs command 1. *Section*. 2. Halt. 3. *Right*. 4. Dress. The even sections oblique to the left, their chiefs commanding, 1 *Forward* in time to add 2. March. 3. *Guide right* the instant each is opposite his place in line. When one yard from the line the chiefs command 1. *Section*. 2. Halt. 3. *Right*. 4. Dress. The chief of each double section superintends the alignment of his double-section, commands *front*, and places himself two yards in front of its center.

The Standard Guard (or standard bearer alone if the "guard" be not with him) obliques to the center of the column between two double sections; or the Standard Bearer hastens to place himself between the two sections in his front (or rear) as they unite; the Senior Aide and Junior Aide taking post on the flanks, or taking command as has just been explained, and as previously may have been directed by the Commander.

If in march, double-sections are formed by the same commands and means except that the even sections are not halted and dressed; the odd sections, instead of halting at section distance, *mark time* at the command of their chiefs, and the chief of each double-section commands, 1. *Forward*, adding 2. March. 3. *Guide left* the instant the sections have joined.

To Break into Sections from Column of Double Sections.

1. *Right by sections.* 2. March. 3. *Guide left.*

At the first command each chief of double-section repeats *Right by section*, and resumes his place in column of sections; the chief of each right section turning his head toward it, but without moving out of his place, commands, *Right section forward*, the chief of each left section in like manner commands: 1. *Left section*. 2. *Mark time*, repeats the command *march*, immediately commands *right oblique*, and adds MARCH, so that each even section may commence the oblique as soon as it is disengaged adding *forward, guide left* when it has gained its place in column.

To Wheel Subdivisions and the Commandery in Circles Consecutively Without Halting.

Being in line.

1. *Threes in circle right* (or *left*) *wheel*. 2. MARCH. 3. *Sections in circle left* (or *right*) *wheel*. 4. MARCH. 5. *Double-sections in circle right* (or *left*) *wheel*. 6. MARCH. 7. *Divisions in circle left* (or *right*) *wheel*. 8. MARCH. 9. *In circle right* (or *left*) *wheel*. 10. MARCH. 11. *Commandery*. 12. HALT. 13. *Left*. 14. DRESS. 15. FRONT; or, 11. *Forward*. 12. *Guide* (*right* or *left*). 13. MARCH.

At the second command each three wheels full about to the right on a fixed pivot. When the circle is nearly completed the third command is given in time to add *march*, the instant the threes are reunited in line and each section, in like manner, wheels on a fixed pivot full about. The Standard Guard so conducts its wheel, on a movable pivot, that it will exactly unite with the sections, as the line is formed each time. When the sections are united in line the second time, that is, having completed the circle, the sixth command is given (the preparatory commands in each case being given so as to add the command of execution as directed). At this command each double-section wheels full about to the right and on a fixed pivot, the Standard Guard wheeling as before but in a larger circle. When the double-sections unite in line as the circles are completed, the eighth command is given and the divisions wheel as described for double-sections, the Standard Guard wheeling as before described. The line being again re-formed, the Commandery is wheeled on a movable pivot by the ninth and tenth commands.

In all the wheelings the command *march* is given the instant the line is re-formed, after the circle is completed, so that the smaller subdivisions re-form the line after the full about, instantly break with the next larger subdivisions, continue the wheelings in the opposite direction and so on.

The Vice-Commanders do not wheel with the subdivisions, but face and march from the center, in prolongation of the line, or close toward it and face to the proper front on the flanks, so that when the half circle is completed, in each wheel, except the last, they with the subdivisions will, for the instant only, be in perfect line faced to the late rear; the Vice-Commanders marking time, the subdivisions continuing the wheel; when they are disengaged the Vice-Commanders face and retrace their steps, again completing the line faced to the original front the instant the full circle is finished, and so on until the wheel is by Commandery front, when they remain on its flank.

This may be executed in part, if desired, omitting such of the wheels as may be deemed expedient or desirable.

To Change Direction of Column, of Sections (Double Sections or Divisions.)

1. *Change direction by the right* (or *left*) *flank.* 2. *Threes right* (or *left*). 3. MARCH.

At the second command the chief of the first section commands, 1. *First section.* 2. *Right forward* 3. *Threes right.*

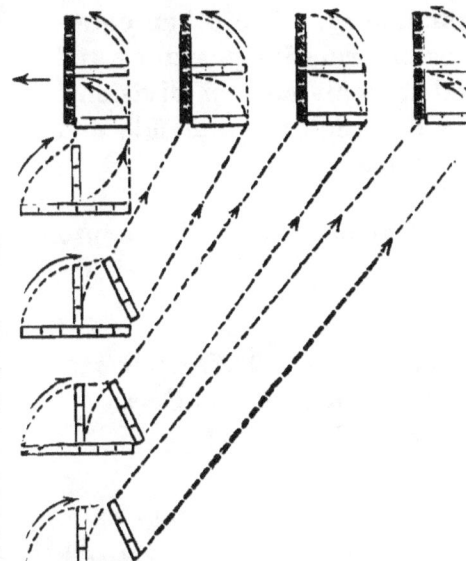

At the command *march* the first section executes *right forward, threes right;* when the rear three completes the wheel to the left the chief commands, 1. *Threes left.* 2. MARCH. 3. *Section.* 4. HALT. 5. *Left.* 6. DRESS. 7. FRONT.

The other sections wheel by threes to the right or half right, and are so conducted by the chiefs as to enter the new column parallel to the first section. As each section arrives in rear of the one next preceding, it is formed in line to the left and dressed to the left. The Vice-Commanders quickly gain their places in the column and assist in the alignment of the guides as heretofore explained.

If the column be of double-sections or divisions, each chief halts in his own person when near the point where the left of his division will rest in column and allows his division to march past him.

To Advance by the Right or Left of Double Sections from Line.

1. *Double-sections.* 2. *Right* (or *left*) *forward.* 3 *Threes right* (or *left*). 4. MARCH. 5. *Guide* (*right* or *left*).

At the third command the First Vice Commander places himself in front of the left file of the right three; the Second Vice-Commander quickly places himself in front of the left file of the right three of the double section on the left of the Commandery. The other chiefs of double sections take the same relative position, and the movement is completed as explained for divisions.

Line or column is formed by similar commands and means as are described for divisions.

To Break by Right of Subdivisions to the Rear into Column.

Being in line at a halt.

1. *Right of sections, rear into column.* 2. *Threes right.* 3. MARCH. 4. *Threes left.* 5. MARCH. 6. *Commandery.* 7 HALT. 8. *Left.* 9. DRESS. 10. FRONT; or 6. *Guide left.*

At the first command the chief of each section cautions the right three that it will have to *right about.* At the third command the threes wheel to the right on fixed pivots. The right three of each section will then change direction to the right (late rear) on a movable pivot, the other threes of each section moving forward and changing direction on the same ground as its right three. The Commander, seeing the movement nearly completed, commands, 4 *Threes left,* in time to add 5. MARCH, the instant the left of the left threes has reached

THE DISPLAY DRILL.

the line lately occupied by the Commandery, and adds, 6. *Commandery.* 7. HALT. The left guides of sections exactly cover each other under direction of the Vice-Commanders and the chiefs of sections; at the tenth command the Vice Commanders take their places in column. If the command for the guide is given the column moves forward without halting.

The Standard Guard wheels about and marches into its place in column, then wheels to the left, regulating its steps so as to maintain its place.

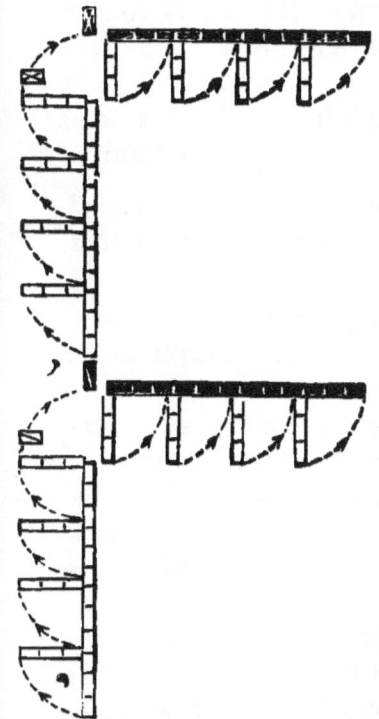

Divisions (or *double-sections*) break to the rear into column from line, by similar commands and means, except that the chiefs of divisions, etc , at the first command, place themselves in front of their divisions and caution the first three as before, repeat the third command, place themselves on the marching flank of the leading three in their division, wheel with it and halt on the late line, so that the file on the marching flanks of the other threes, in passing to the rear, will graze the chief's right arm. When the rear three nearly completes the wheel each chief of division (or double-section) commands, 4. *Threes left.* 5. MARCH. 6. *Division* (or *double section*). 7. HALT; the left guide of the division places himself so that his left arm will lightly touch the chief's breast, who then gives the eighth, ninth and tenth commands (in lieu of Commander, as explained for the same movement by section), and places himself in front of the center of his division or double-section.

Similar movements by files without the wheelings of threes, being at a halt, are made thus:

1. *Right of sections rear into column.* 2 *Right.* 3. FACE. 4. *Forward.* 5. MARCH. 6. *Commandery.* 7. HALT. 8. *Left* 9. FACE. 10. *Left.* 11. DRESS. 12. FRONT; or, 6. *By the left flank* 7. MARCH. 8 *Guide left.*

At the third command the Knights at the right of sections (chiefs) come to an *about face,* and at the fifth command move straight to the rear; the others follow, turning on the same ground. When the last Knight or file is about to turn to the rear the Commander halts the Commandery, faces it to the left, and dresses it as explained, or marches it by the left flank into column.

1. *Right of sections rear into column.* 2. *By the right flank.* 3. MARCH 4 *By the left flank* 5. MARCH. 6. *Guide left.* Being in line marching.

At the third command the right file of each section executes *to the rear, march,* and marches straight to the rear; the others face and march to the right. On arriving at the point where the right file marched to the rear, each file of that section in succession follows in his trace, being careful to keep closed to facing distance, each section executing the same movement at the same instant. The fifth command is given the instant the last files are about to turn to the rear, so that they do not in fact turn but continue to march straight forward; or the command may be delayed until he turns to the rear so that all march by the left flank at that command.

THE DISPLAY DRILL. 117

The officers take their positions as heretofore explained.

Divisions and double sections are formed into column by files from the right of divisions to the rear, by similar commands and means.

To Deploy Column of Double Sections.

Being at a halt.

1. *On first double-section deploy column* 2. *Threes left (or right).* 3. MARCH. 4. FRONT.

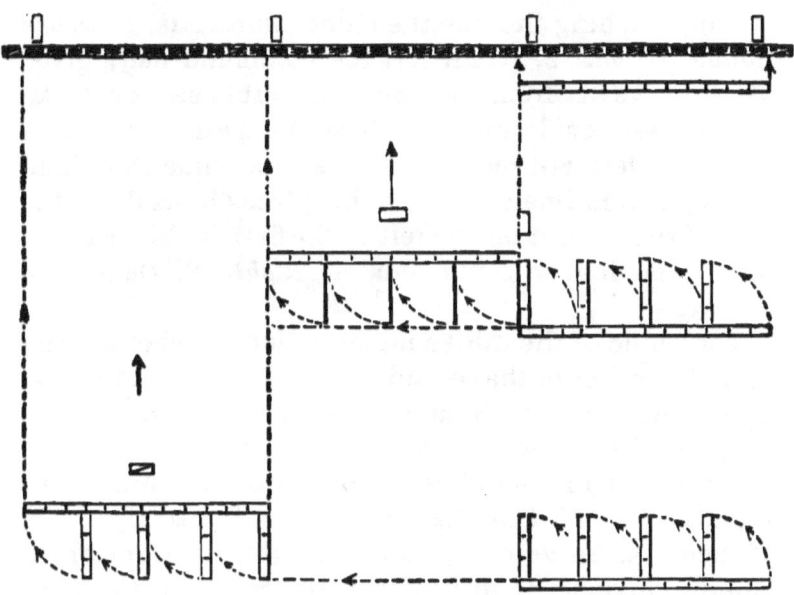

At the first command the chief of the first double-section cautions it to *stand fast*, and places himself three yards in front of his place on the right; the left guide steps three yards straight to the front; the other chiefs repeat *threes left* and quickly place themselves two yards in front of the left guides facing the left. At the command *march* the chief of the first double-section commands, 1. *First double-section* 2. *Right.* 3. Dress. 4. Front; at the third command it dresses on the line between the chief and left guide.

The other double sections wheel by threes to the left, the chiefs repeating the command to *march*

The chief of the second double-section stands fast, and when the left of his double-section approaches him, commands, 1. *Second double-section.* 2. *Threes right.* 3. March. 4. *Guide right.* The third command is given the instant the front rank of the rear three (if there be two ranks, or if not, then when the rear three) arrives opposite the place of the right file when in line. On approaching the line the chief commands, 1. *Second double section.* 2. Halt. At the command *halt*, given at three yards from the line, the double section halts, and its left guide quickly places himself on the line where its left will rest, and at the same time the chief, if his place in line is on its right, places himself at the side of the Knight on the left of the first double-section, and immediately commands, 1. *Right.* 2. Dress. 3. Front.

The guide of the third double-section marches abreast of and parallel to the second; its chief having advanced two yards, after the command *threes right march* by the chief of the second, halts in his own person, and when the right of his double-section approaches him commands, 1. *Third double-section.* 2. *Threes right.* 3 March. 4. *Guide right*, and, marching in front of its center, conducts it to within three yards of the line, when he halts and dresses it to the right, as just explained for the second double-section.

THE DISPLAY DRILL. 119

If there are more than three double-sections the others execute the movement as described for the second and third

If marching the chief of the first double-section halts it at the command *march*, and the movement is executed as before

1. *On third double-section deploy column.* 2. *Threes right* (or *left*) 3 MARCH.

Being at a halt.

At the second command the chief of the third double-section cautions it to stand fast.

At the command *march* all the double sections, except the third, wheel by threes to the right, the chiefs repeating the second and third commands; the chief of

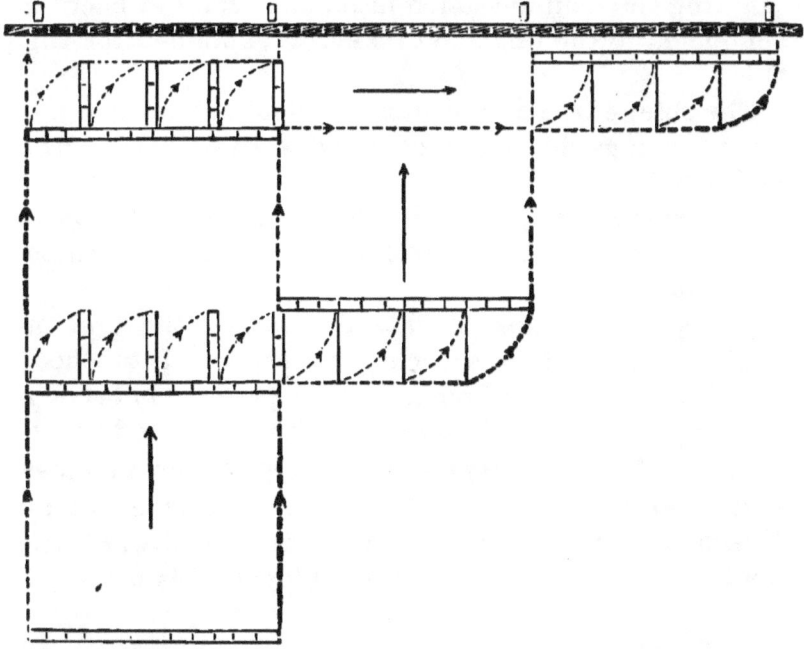

the first double section conducts his double-section to the right in prolongation of its former front; the chief of the section halts opposite the right of the third, **and** when the rear of his double section approaches, commands, 1. *Second double section.* 2. *Threes left.* 3. MARCH. 4 *Double-section.* 5. HALT. Third command is given the instant the third double-section is unmasked.

The chief of the third double-section when he sees it nearly unmasked, commands, 1. *Third double section.* 2. *Forward.* 3. *Guide left.* 4 MARCH When this double section reaches the ground from which the first one moved to the right, the chief commands 1 *Third double-section* 2. HALT. At the command *halt* the chief and left guide quickly place themselves three yards in front of their places in line, and the chief commands:

1 *Third double section.* 2. *Left* 3. DRESS. 4. FRONT

If there are more than three double-sections each conforms to what is explained for the second but unmasking the double-section in its late rear and each is conducted to the line and dressed as explained for the third.

The chief of the first, dresses his double-section to the left as soon as the command *front* is given to the second double-section.

If in march the chief of the third double section halts it at the command *march*, the movement is executed as before.

To deploy the column faced to the rear on the first or third double-section without first causing it to wheel about by threes, the Commander adds, *faced to the rear* after *deploy column.* The movement is executed as already explained, except each double-section marches three yards beyond the line, then wheels about by threes and halts, after which it is dressed toward the double section upon which the deployment is made.

Deployments on Interior Double-sections.

1. *On* (such) *double-section* (*division* or *Standard Guard*) *deploy column.* 2. *Threes right and left.* 3. March.

At the command *march* the double-sections in front of the one designated, deploy to the right; those in rear deploy to the left. The designated double-section, as soon as unmasked, is conducted on the line of the first double-section, with the guide right, and is dressed to the right. The other double-sections are dressed toward the designated double section.

To Deploy Column of Threes in Open Order.
Being in march.

1. *On right three* (so many yards) *take distance.* 2 March.

At the second command the leading three marches straight forward; the others *halt.* When the second three has gained six yards (if the number is not given in the command) from the three in front, it resumes the full step at the command *forward, march,* by its chief, and so on in succession to the rear of the column.

The Commander then commands:

1. *On center deploy.* 2. March. 3. *Guide center.*

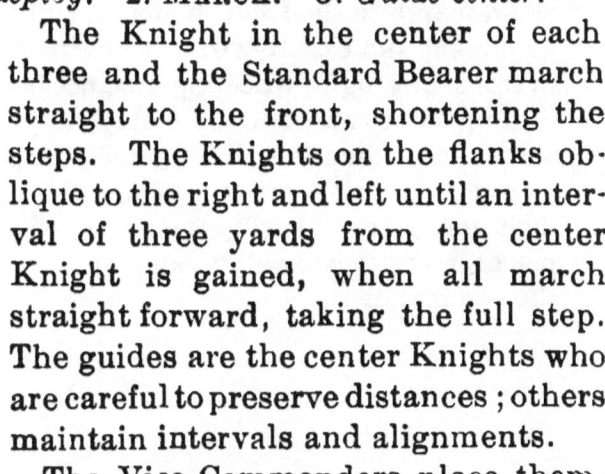

The Knight in the center of each three and the Standard Bearer march straight to the front, shortening the steps. The Knights on the flanks oblique to the right and left until an interval of three yards from the center Knight is gained, when all march straight forward, taking the full step. The guides are the center Knights who are careful to preserve distances; others maintain intervals and alignments.

The Vice-Commanders place themselves in front and rear of the center leading or following the guides, and three yards (or one-half the given distance) from the advance and rearmost three.

To Deploy Column of Sections, etc.

Distance from the right is gained as just explained.

1. *On right* (or *left*) *center deploy*. 2. **March.**
3. *Guide center.*

The movement is executed as in column of threes, except that the Knights on the right of the center, according to the command, march straight forward, the others oblique right and left as commanded. The Standard Bearer marches forward so as to occupy, as near as practicable, the center of the column; the Senior Aid and Junior Aid oblique to the right and left to the given interval. The Vice-Commanders are in front and rear of the center as before, and on a line between them is the standard. The guides are the Knights on whom, or from whom the deployment was made.

To Close the Column Again.

1 *To full distance close column and intervals.* 2. **March.**

The Knights on the flanks oblique toward the center and when they have gained their places in threes (or other subdivisions from which deployment was made), again march to the front, being careful to preserve the alignment and exactly cover the corresponding Knights in front, closing to wheeling distance immediately; the leading threes shorten the steps, as do each three in succession, when they have gained the proper distance. At the command *forward. march*, all resume the thirty-inch step; the Vice Commanders also regain their places, so as to be ready to step off with the column at the command.

THE DISPLAY DRILL. 123

To Close on the Center only

Without disturbing the distance between the threes the Commander commands:

    1. *On center close intervals.* 2. MARCH.

The Knights gradually regain their positions on the center, re-forming threes, by oblique steps gaining ground forward, keeping the shoulders square to the front and maintaining the alignments.

To Close Threes to Wheeling Distance.

Before or after closing the intervals between the Knights of each three the Commander commands:

1. *To wheeling* (or such) *distance close column.* 2. MARCH.

The files in front shorten their steps, and when the threes are closed to the designated distance, as before explained, the Commander commands *forward, march,* and all take the thirty-inch step.

If the command be *double time* the leading three continues the march in *quick time,* those in rear close in *double time,* until having gained the distance indicated, each in succession marches in quick time, taking the step from the guide in front.

To Deploy Line by Files to the Front.

1. *On standard (right* or *left file) deploy;* 2. MARCH.
    or, 2. *Double time.* 3. MARCH.

At the second command the Standard Bearer advances by short steps straight to the front; the Knights on his right oblique to the right, those on his left oblique to the left until each in succession has gained an interval of three yards from the standard or the Knight next to them toward the Standard Bearer when they turn and march to the front dressing toward the center, which should never be passed. When all have arrived in line the Commander commands, *forward, march*, and all take the full step.

If the command be *double time* the Standard Bearer advances with the full step; the others oblique as described, but in double time, taking the step from the Standard Bearer as they arrive on the line.

To Deploy Line in Open Order by the Flank.

1. *By the right* (or *left*) *flank take intervals.* 2. March. 3. *Commandery.* 4. Halt; or, 3. *By the left* (or *right*) *flank.* 4. March. 5. *Guide right* (*left* or *center*)

Being in line, single rank.

At the second command the Commandery faces to the right and if in march, halts; the First Vice-Commander alone continues the march in prolongation of the former line the others follow successively at the distance of three yards, each steadily in trace of his predecessor until the Knight, or Second Vice-Commander in rear of the column has the interval when at the fourth command all halt pause the nineteenth of a minute, and face to the former front Or,

The line is re-formed and moves to the front, at the command *by the left flank, march.*

1 *On Standard* (*right* or *left center*). 2. *By the right and left flanks take intervals.* 3 March. 4 *Commandery.* 5 Halt; or, 4. *By the left and right flanks.* 5. March. 6 *Guide center* (*right* or *left*).

Being in line single rank.

The Commander points with his sword to the center file on which the movement is to be made, and at the third command those on its right face to the right; those on its left face to left, and the movement is executed upon the principles before explained.

To Extend Intervals.

1. *By the right* (or *left*) *flank to* (so many) *yards extend intervals.* 2. MARCH. 3. *Commandery.* 4 HALT; or, 3. *By the left* (or *right*) *flank.* 4. MARCH.

The movement is executed as before explained.

If desired to deploy from line or column to a greater interval than three yards, the number of yards is stated in the command and the movement is executed on the same principles.

To Close the Intervals by the Flank.

1. *By the left* (or *right*) *flank close intervals.* 2 MARCH.

At the command *march* the left guide stands fast (or if in march, halts) the others march by the left flank and successively halt and face to the front upon closing to their places.

To March Files to the Rear from Column of Threes at Open Order (Deployed).

Being in march.

1. *To the rear.* 2 MARCH. Or,

1. *Counter-march* 2. *By files right* (or *left*). 3. MARCH.

At the second command the First Vice-Commander faces to the right, and having arrived opposite the center, between numbers one and two, again faces to the right and marches to the rear. As he turns to the rear the Commander commands *march*, at which the leading number two faces to the right, and when in rear of the First Vice Commander turns and follows in his trace; number three of the leading three turns to the right, and when he arrives at a point half way between the place from which he turned and the place just occupied by number two, he faces and marches to the rear. . Number one executes the same movements, turning to the rear when he has gained ground to the right equal to one-half the distance between his own position and that of number two before the movement commenced. The others advance and follow exactly in trace of their fraters in front, turning on the same ground.

The alignment and intervals should be carefully preserved. The movement to the left is similarly executed.

Order in Echelon.

Being in line at a halt, (or in march).

1. *Threes* (or *sections*) *on center* (*right* or *left*), *front into echelon.* 2 MARCH. 3. *Guide center* (*right* or *left*).

At the first command the Senior Aid cautions the Standard Guard to 1. *Forward.* 2. *Guide center*, and the chiefs of other threes caution *stand fast* (or *halt*), at the command MARCH the Standard Guard marches straight forward; when it has advanced fifty-four inches the threes next on its right and left, at the caution of their chiefs given in a low tone, take up the march, and so on until the entire line is in march.

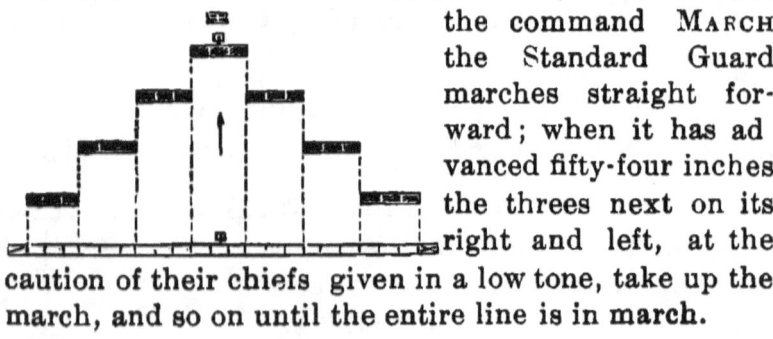

The Knight on the right and left of each three toward the center is the guide of his three, and is careful to preserve the designated distance from the standard or preceding three, and exactly opposite his place in line, as well as to keep dressed on the three opposite to him.

The Vice-Commanders also take up the march at the prescribed distance, and the Commander places himself in front of the standard at the same distance, or may march in rear of the standard on a line with the Vice-Commanders.

If the Commander desires the distance to be greater or less he adds to the first command, after the word "center" *at* (so many) *yards distance*, and the movement is similarly executed.

Sections in echelon is similarly executed.

1. *Threes* (or *files*) *on right* (or *left*) *of divisions front into echelon.* 2. MARCH. 3. *Guide right* (or *left*).

Being in line.

Each division executes the movement as explained for the Commandery, the right three of each division marching forward at the second command; the second three of each division moving forward as explained when the first has gained fifty-four inches and so on. The first Vice-Commander places himself on the right of the leading three of the first division; the Second Vice-Commander quickly places himself on the left and abreast of the rear three of the left division.

The Standard Guard maintains its place in the center abreast of the leading threes.

To March in Echelon to the Rear.

1 *Threes right* (or *left*) *about.* 2. MARCH. 3. *Guide* (*right* or *left*).

The Vice-Commanders wheel as number three of a rank of three into their places *in echelon.*

To March in Echelon by the Flank.

1. *Threes right* (or *left*). 2. MARCH. 3. *Guide* (*right, left* or *center*).

The Vice-Commanders wheel so as to gain the same relative position when the movement is completed.

Sections may be wheeled to the right or left, changing direction in echelon.

To Re-form the Line.

1. *On center* (or such a subdivision) *front into line.* 2. MARCH. 3. *Center.* 4. DRESS.

At the first command the Senior Aid, or chief of the leading subdivision, cautions it that it will have to halt; the chiefs of other threes or subdivisions, to the right and left in rear of the center, command *forward*, and repeat the command *march*, at the same time the Senior Aid, or chief of the leading subdivisions, commands it to halt; the three on each side of the center halt and dress toward the center on arriving in rear of the line, so that the threes opposite each other *in echelon* will halt and dress at the same instant. When the last has dressed the Commander commands *front.*

To Form Sections in Echelon from Threes in Echelon.

Threes being in march at four yards distance in echelon command:

1. *Odd threes in circles right wheel.* 2. MARCH.

At the command *march* the first, third and other odd threes wheel to the right, on fixed pivots, completing a full about; the even threes continue the march and unite in sections with the odd threes the instant they have completed the circle, and the sections move forward in echelon without halting. The sections may be wheeled by similar commands and means forming double-sections in echelon, which may also be wheeled in like manner forming divisions, and so on, until the line is formed, each Knight and Subdivision regulating the step, so as to give or retain his proper place.

To Form in Echelon from Column of Files.

Being in march, double ranks.

1. *Files right and left into echelon.* 2. MARCH.

At the command *march* the two leading Knights place themselves about one foot apart, and then by short steps march straight forward; the other left files oblique to the left, and each in succession will resume the forward, without command, when his right shoulder shall exactly cover the left shoulder of the Knight next in front. The right files gain ground to the right in a similar manner, the left shoulder of each exactly covering the right shoulder of the Knight next in front. The Standard Guard forms in line and marks time at command of its chief until it gains its proper place in the center and on a line with the rearmost Knights (Vice-Commanders) in the column; the First Vice Commander quickly places himself at the right and rear of the right column, and the Second Vice-Commander at the left and rear of the left column of files *in echelon.*

The Commander commands *forward*, adding MARCH the instant the movement is completed, and places himself in front of the leading files

If the lines are small, ground is gradually gained to the right and left, the Knights keeping the shoulders square to the front, as they may have been previously instructed by the Commander; or he may indicate it by giving as the first command, *files bear right and left into echelon*.

To Re-form Column of Files.

1. *Files.* 2. *Right and left into column.* 3. MARCH.

At the first command the First Vice-Commander takes his place at the head of the column.

The leading Knight advances by shortened steps; the others oblique toward the center, regulating the steps so that each double file will successively reunite, then, turning to the front, will follow in trace of those immediately in their lead. The Standard Guard marches forward to its place.

To Open and Close Ranks in Echelon from Line.

1. *By turns.* 2. *Threes front into echelon.* 3. MARCH.

At the third command, given as the right foot strikes the ground, the left threes of each section *mark time*, the right threes advance until the right foot has been planted the third time (*i. e.*, six steps), when they too mark time; the rear threes having planted the right foot the third time, step off with the left foot, pass between the threes in their front, and advance six steps in front of them, being twelve steps from their first position, when they mark time again, and so on by turns until the Commander desires the line to advance together, when he commands, 1. *Forward.* 2. *Guide right* (or *left*). 3. MARCH; the third command being given the instant the line is re formed

THE DISPLAY DRILL. 131

The Vice-Commanders successively advance with the threes in front.

———   ———   ———   —

——   ——   ——

Or, he commands, *Odd threes in circle right wheel*, adding MARCH the instant the line is formed, when the odd threes wheel full about; the even threes march between the wheeling threes, which advance as soon as they complete the circle.

If the Commander desires the threes to march in column, he commands *threes right* (or *left*) in time to add *march* the instant the threes are united in line. Or the line may be halted the instant it is reunited and is dressed by the usual commands.

General Remarks, Apropos.

In the formations of figures, etc., no rigid rules can be given, as the number of officers or Knights, the presence of the Standard Bearer alone, or of the full guard would necessitate some modification in each case by the officer in charge, or interminable explanations in the tactics.

The *commands* of the chiefs of threes are in fact merely cautions to enable the threes to move together, and may be dispensed with if so instructed by the Commander. *This rule is general* and may be applied to sections at the discretion of the officer in charge.

To Form Cross from Column of Threes.

Being in march, single rank.

1. *Form cross.* 2. March. 3. *Forward.* 4. March, 5. *Guide center.*

At the second command the First Vice-Commander 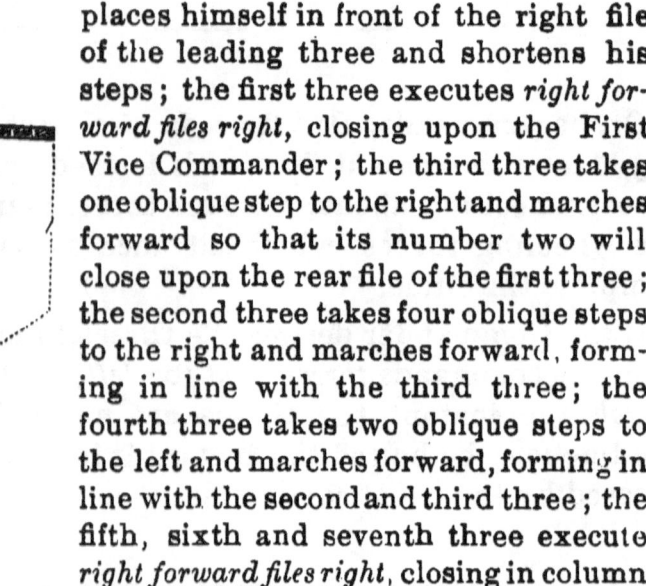 places himself in front of the right file of the leading three and shortens his steps; the first three executes *right forward files right,* closing upon the First Vice Commander; the third three takes one oblique step to the right and marches forward so that its number two will close upon the rear file of the first three; the second three takes four oblique steps to the right and marches forward, forming in line with the third three; the fourth three takes two oblique steps to the left and marches forward, forming in line with the second and third three; the fifth, sixth and seventh three execute *right forward files right,* closing in column of files upon number two of the third three. The threes shorten their steps upon arriving in their places. The Second Vice Commander follows in rear of the column. Seeing the movement completed the Commander gives the concluding commands, and places himself at the head of the cross.

The length of the steps is regulated so as to bring the threes into their proper places.

If there be but five threes the movement is similarly executed, the third three forming the left arm of the cross

If there are eight threes, with the Standard Guard in the column, the first and second threes form the upper arm of the cross; the third three obliques to the right; the fourth three obliques to the left; the Standard Guard obliques twenty-two inches to the right, and marches straight forward; the four threes in rear form the lower arm of the cross upon principles explained before At the command *march* the First Vice Commander quickly places himself on the right of the third three, and the Second Vice commander quickly places himself on the left of the fourth three; so that the Vice-Commanders will be on the flanks of the horizontal arm of the cross and the standard at the angles in its center. The Commander marches about four yards to the left and abreast of the Second Vice Commander or at the top as before.

Cross from column of sections is formed by similar commands and means.

Supernumerary threes close in column as the base of the cross, or may form in triangle. etc., as hereafter explained, the command being, 2. *Rear threes form triangle*, etc.

To Reduce Cross to Column.

Of like subdivisions from which it was formed
 1. *Form column.* 2. March 3 *Guide left.*

At the command *march* the threes that are in column of files execute the *left front into line,* the first three continues the march; the second three *left obliques* into column the third three *marks time,* until it is disengaged when it obliques into its place in column; the fourth three *right obliques* to its place. The threes having reformed the column *mark time,* when their guides are in trace of the guide in front, and successively advance as each gains its distance.

The Commander gives the third command as soon as the movement is completed.

To Form Greek Cross from Column of Sections, etc.

The arms of a Greek Cross are so nearly equal that the difference is not readily perceived. The same number of threes sections, etc , form each arm of the cross; usually the Standard Guard is in the center, the First Vice Commander at the top (in advance), and the Second Vice-Commander in rear at the base. These may be changed when necessary to equalize the limbs of the cross.

1. *Form Greek Cross.* 2. MARCH. 3. *Guide center.*

At the first command the sections execute the following movements, the chiefs giving the commands if necessary to insure prompt action; First and fourth sections, *right forward files right*, forming the advance and rear arms of the cross; second section and Standard Guard, *right oblique*, forming the right arm and center; third section *left oblique*, forming the left arm, as described before for the Passion Cross

Greek Cross from column of threes and double sections is formed by similar means, the chiefs giving the commands for their double-sections, causing them to take the short step, to march forward, etc., at the proper time. As the cross is completed the chiefs promptly take their places and the cross moves forward at the command of the Commander.

To Reduce Greek Cross to Column.

From which it was formed, command,

1. *Form column.* 2. MARCH. 3. *Guide left.*

At the first command the following movements are executed as indicated by the command, viz.:

First and fourth sections. *Left front into line.*
Second section and Standard Guard. *Left oblique.*
Third section *Right oblique.*
And the movement is completed as explained for the Passion Cross.

To Form Greek and Passion Cross from Column of Threes.

The Vice-Commanders, Standard Guard and eight threes being in the column marching

1. *Form Cross.* 2. *Leading threes form Greek Cross.* 3. **March.** 4. *Guide center.*

At the command *march* the four threes, nearest to the head of the column, form Greek Cross; the first and fourth threes executing *right forward files right;* the second three obliques to the right and the third three obliques to the left, forming the several arms of the cross, as before explained the First Vice-Commander quickly placing himself in its center; the Senior Aide places himself forty-four inches to the front and shortens his steps; the Standard Bearer quickly takes the place thus vacated, and the Junior Aid places himself between the two; the Second Vice Commander quickly places himself in front of the Senior

Aid, and the cross is formed as before explained with the standard in its center.

The Commander places himself at the head of the Passion Cross and commands *forward,* MARCH, and all move forward.

Care should be taken to preserve the proper distance between the two crosses, which will result from the same step being taken by the Knight at the head of each.

The cross is reduced by commands and means similar to those before explained.

Supernumerary threes may form at the base as shown in illustration (2), or may form a second Greek Cross. In the latter case the second command would be, 2. *Leading and rear threes form, etc.*

The crosses are reduced by the commands, etc., as before.

To Display Greek Cross and Reduce it to Column again.

Being in column marching

1. *Display Greek Cross.* 2. MARCH. 3. *Guide center.*

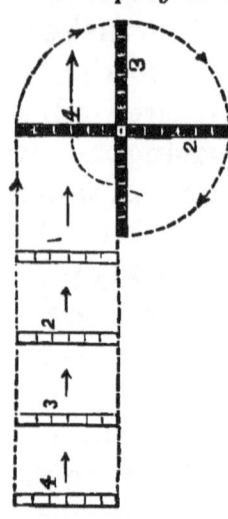

At the command *march* the First Vice-Commander continues the march full two yards straight forward and halts; the leading section wheels to the right (or left, according to previous instructions) in a complete circle, the pivot Knight taking short steps, so as to describe a circle of about one yard in diameter; the three sections in its rear, march forward until each in succession has gained the ground from which the first section commenced the wheel, when each wheels, following exactly in trace of the preceding section. The chief of the leading section commands *forward*, in a low tone, in time to add *march* the instant it has gained the ground from which it commenced the wheel, and this section marches straight to the front; the others follow it in column from the same point. These commands should be loud enough to be heard only by the section to whom they are addressed, that the cross may appear to dissolve without command.

The guide is then on the same flank that it was before the movement commenced, and without command

The Second Vice Commander places himself on the left of the fifth section, and during the display, the rear sections *halt* at his command, given the instant before the fourth section commences, and resume the forward march when that section completes the wheel, so that they may not be too close during the display of the cross, and may move forward and keep the proper dis tance as soon as it is reduced.

The sections, in wheeling, form right angles with each other, and the alignment must be perfect.

If the Standard Guard is between either of these four sections, it obliques to the center as soon as the section in its front is about to commence the wheel and quickly forms a close group facing each other (inward), the standard supported in the center by the three; it resumes its place in column when the same section begins the forward march. If so instructed the Standard Bearer may be detached and, alone with the standard, occupy the center of the cross; or the Commander or First Vice-Commander may do so.

If there are eight sections (or threes) two crosses may be displayed at the same instant and in the same manner the First Vice-Commander filling the center of the leading cross, the Second Vice-Commander that of the one in its rear, the Standard obliques to the center, between the two crosses, and halts, Or, the rear sections form square, triangle, etc . and reduce them as the cross is reduced. These combinations are numerous, and when well executed have a fine effect It is not so well, however, in the *display* as in the *formation* of Greek and other crosses.

The object in wheeling to the right is that the left guides may be on the marching flanks. If so instructed, the cross may be displayed to the left, and in absence of the Standard Guard the Commander, with the Vice Commanders, may place themselves in the center, back to back, thus : .·. Or, either of them alone may occupy the center. They resume their places in column as soon as the leading section commences the *forward*

To Form Greek Cross from Line.

1. *Form Greek Cross.* 2. March. 3. *Forward.* 4. March. 5. *Guide center.*

Four sections being in line, marching, with the Standard Guard in the center

At the first command the officers command as follows:

First Vice Commander—1. *First section* 2. *Threes left.*

Second Vice-Commander—1. *Fourth section.* 2. *To the rear.* 3. *Threes left.*

Senior Aid — 1. *Center sections and Standard Guard.* 2. *Mark time.*

At the command *march*, given as the right foot is coming to the ground, the first section wheels by threes, on movable pivots, to the left and marches in column of threes, parallel to the front of the second section, toward the center; the center sections and Standard Guard *mark time;* the fourth section executes *to the rear, march,* and immediately wheels by threes, on movable pivots, to the left, then marches in column of threes across the rear of the third section to the center. When the leading three of the first section reaches the front of the Standard Bearer it executes *by the right flank march,* and marks time; the original first three obliques to the right, and in like manner forms column of files in front of its second three thus completing the upper limb of the cross, with the First Vice-Commander at the top.

The leading (being the first) three of the fourth section forms column of files in rear of the Standard Bearer, by executing *by the left flank,* and *marking time;* the second three of the fourth section *right obliques* to the rear of its first three and executes *by the left flank,* forming with it the lower limb of the cross, with the Second Vice-Commander in its rear.

The Commander gives the fourth command, and the cross moves forward.

If so instructed, the flank sections may wheel by section and form the upper and lower parts of the cross without breaking by threes, and the commands of the Vice-Commanders are changed accordingly to 1. *First section.* 2. *Left wheel,* etc.

Similar formations are made by double sections, threes, etc., to form Passion or other crosses, with or without the Standard Guard.

To Reduce Greek Cross to Line.

1. *Form line.* 2. March. 3. *Forward.* 4. March.
5. *Guide right* (or *left*).

At the first command the First Vice-Commander placing himself on its right, commands: 1. *First section.* 2. *By the right flank.*

Second Vice-Commander, placing himself on its left; 1. *Fourth section.* 2. *By the left flank.* Senior Aid: 1. *Center sections and Standard Guard.* 2. *Mark time.*

At the command *march* the first section executes *by the right flank*, forming line, and is conducted by the First Vice-Commander to the right of the second section, caused to wheel on a movable pivot to the right, then executes *to the rear, march* and *marks time* in its place on the right of the line; in the meantime the lower limb of the cross (fourth section) executes *by the left flank*, is conducted by the Second Vice-Commander to the left of third section, and caused to *right wheel*, (on a movable pivot) to its place on the left.

The Vice-Commanders take their places on the right and left as soon as their sections have gained their positions, and the Commander immediately commands *forward,* etc.

If desired, the cross is reduced into column of sections as before explained; or cross, formed from column of sections, may be reduced into line, as just explained.

To Form Patriarchal Cross.

Being in column of threes.

1. *Form Patriarchal Cross.* 2. MARCH. 3. *Forward.* 4. MARCH. 5. *Guide center.*

At the second command the first three executes *right forward files right* and takes the short step, when its leading file has advanced two steps; the fourth, fifth and eighth threes execute the same movement and close upon the first three in column of files; the second three obliques to the right and marches forward, forming the right half of the horizontal limb of the cross, as explained for cross, with number one of the fourth three on its left; the third three obliques to the left, then marches forward, and with the second three and number one of the fourth three, forms the upper horizontal arms of the cross; the sixth three executes the movement as described for the second three, forming the right half (or arm) of the lower horizontal portion of the cross, with number three of the fifth three; the seventh three executes the movement described for the third three, forming in line with the sixth three and number three of the fifth three; the Vice-Commanders place themselves on the right and left flanks of the lower horizontal limbs; and the Commander gives the fourth command and places himself at the head of the cross.

[If the Standard Guard is present the Standard Bearer quickly places himself in the center of one of the horizontal portions of the cross; the Senior Aid and Junior Aid taking the outer flanks or move with the Standard Bearer; the Vice-Commanders leading and following the column, and the Commander marches four yards from the left flank and abreast of the leading horizontal line. These various positions are determined by the number in rank in order to preserve the proper proportions of the cross, and upon principles explained.

Cross is formed from column of sections, etc., by similar commands and means.

To Reduce Patriarchal Cross.

1. *Form column.* 2. MARCH. 3. *Guide left.*

This is executed by means similar to the reduction of the Passion Cross, before explained.

To Form Cross of Salem.

Being in column of threes.

1. *Form Cross of Salem.* 2. MARCH. 3. *Guide center.*

Cross of Salem is a Patriachal Cross, with an additional cross at its base, like the one at the top, and is formed by similar means; the rear cross forming, as has been explained for the upper part of patriarchal Cross, closing up and uniting with the lower limb of the Patriarchal Cross.

The officers take their places, so as to effect the proper proportions of the different limbs of the cross, depending upon the number of threes (or sections) in the column.

To Reduce Cross of Salem.

1. *Form column.* 2. MARCH. 3. *Guide left.*

The cross is reduced by means similar to the reduction of other crosses, as before explained.

To Form Cross of St Andrew from Column of Divisions or Double Sections.

1. *Form Cross of St. Andrew.* 2 *Left and right half wheel.* 3. MARCH. 4. *Right and left oblique.* 5. MARCH. 6. *Forward.* 7. MARCH. 8. *Guide center.*

THE DISPLAY DRILL.

At the second command the First Vice-Commander commands: 1. *First division* [or *double section*, etc] 2. *Left and right, inward, half wheel.* Second Vice-Commander—1. *Second division.* 2. *Right and left, outward, half wheel*

At the command *march* the leading division (half) wheels inwardly on fixed pivots, forming a letter **V**; the second division (half) wheels outwardly on movable pivots, forming an inverted **∧**; the Standard Bearer retains his place, at the angle of the leading **V**, and the Senior Aid and Junior Aid place themselves abreast twelve inches in his rear and about six inches apart.

The Commander gives the fourth command in time to add *march* the instant the half wheels are completed; at which the leading division faces to its former front and shortens the step a little; the second division faces in the same direction, and advancing obliquely toward the center without deranging the positions of the shoulders, closes the interval between its leading files and the distance between them and the Standard Guard, so as to form a letter **X** with the Standard Bearer in its center The Vice-Commanders quickly place themselves, in echelon, at the heads of the cross (the First Vice-Commander on the right), which marches with full step to its present front, late front of the column, at command of the Commander, who places himself in front of the Standard and on a line with the Vice Commanders.

If there be no Standard Guard the Commander occupies the center, and the Vice Commanders take the Senior Aid's and Junior Aid's places.

To Reduce Cross of St. Andrew.

1. *Form column.* 2. *Right and left front into line.* 3. MARCH. 4. *Guide left.*

At the second command the officers quickly place themselves in front of the several arms of the cross and command:

First Vice-Commander—(To upper right arm). 1. *First section.* 2. *Left front into line.*

Second Vice-Commander—(To lower left arm.) 1. *Fourth section.* 2. *Left front into line.*

Senior Aid—(To lower right arm). 1. *Third section.* 2. *Right front into line.*

Junior Aid—(To upper left arm). 1. *Second section.* 2 *Mark time.*

[If the arms of the cross are more or less than a section, change the command to suit, thus: " Right wing, first division. Left front into line," etc.]

At the command *march* the several sections of the cross execute the commands, and the leading section, having formed line, marches forward at the command of the First Vice Commander; as soon as the second section is unmasked it executes *right front into line* at command of the Junior Aid, and by his command obliques into its place in column. The other sections are marched into their places by similar commands and means, regulating the step so as to immediately gain their position in column, and the officers take their places.

TRIANGLES.

From Column of Files Single Rank

Station two markers two yards apart opposite each other, near the apex, and one at each angle at the base of triangle to be formed. The column being in march, command:

1. *Form triangle.* 2 *Column half left and right.* 3. MARCH.

The third command is given when the column is about three yards from the markers at the apex.

The First Vice-Commander conducts the column *half left*, parallel to the line of the markers on that side, halts his division when its head has reached the point opposite the place where it will rest, and faces it to the right; the Senior Aid follows, conducting his center division until nearing the point where the first division inclined to the left, when he marches it *column half left* in rear of the first division, beyond the marker at the head of the first division, marches it *column right* three yards in rear of and opposite the base of the triangle, halts and faces it to the right; the Second Vice-Commander follows, with the third division, to the ground from which the first division changed direction, then by *column half right* marches it parallel to the line of markers on that side, halts it opposite its place, and causes it to *left face.*

Each chief, having faced his division toward the center, as soon as it arrives opposite to its place, takes his post (the Vice-Commanders at the apex of the triangle and the Aids on the flanks of their division); each dresses his division up to the line toward himself, against the marker. leaving room for the Commander to form the apex of the triangle.

The Junior Aid hastens to place himself in front of the second division, when it first changes direction, near the apex of the triangle.

To Reduce the Triangle.

1. *Column of files.* 2. *Right and left.* 3. Face. 4. *Forward.* 5. March.

At the second command the First Vice-Commander and Senior Aid command: 1. —— *division.* 2 *Right,* the Second Vice Commander, 1. *Third division.* 2. *Left,* and the chiefs repeat the third command. At the command *forward,* the First Vice Commander commands, 1. *First division.* 2. *Stand fast.* At *march* the Second Vice-Commander conducts his division back, left in front, over the ground it traversed in forming the triangle, the Senior Aid conducts the second division past the rear of the first division, retracing its steps to the point where it executed *column half left,* and there unites in column of files with and in rear of the Second Vice-Commander's division, and resumes his own place (the Junior Aid takes his place as soon as the second division commences the forward march); the First Vice-Commander causes his division to move forward in rear of and uniting with the second division as it passes, and takes his place in rear of the column.

When the divisions are joined in column of files the Commander halts and faces it to the right continues the march left in front, or he commands *to the rear, march,* or uses such other method to bring the right in front as he desires.

To Form Triangle from Column of Threes about a Grave or Delta.

1. *Form triangle.* 2. *Column half right and left.* 3. MARCH.

If the Standard Guard occupies the center of the column, the Senior Aid and Junior Aid immediately place themselves in front and rear of the center column, and at the command *march*, the two left divisions (columns) march together, *column half left*, and the right division marches *column half right*, conducted by their chiefs to their places, as before.

To Reduce the Triangle.

1. *Column of threes.* 2 *Right and left.* 3. FACE. 4 *Forward.* 5. MARCH.

The divisions step off together, retrace their steps, conducted by their chiefs, and each is halted when its rear reaches the ground from which it changed direction at the apex of the triangle to march out of the column. The Junior Aid takes his place in the second division as soon as it commences the forward march; the chiefs of division resume their places as the column is re-formed.

If it be desired to form column of files, the commands are given as before explained, and the movement is similarly executed.

To Form Triangle from Column of Threes.

Being in march.

1. *To half distance close column.* 2. MARCH.

Executed as before explained.

THE DISPLAY DRILL.

1. *Form triangle.* 2. MARCH.

At the first command the Junior Aid hastens to place himself in rear of the rear file of the middle column; 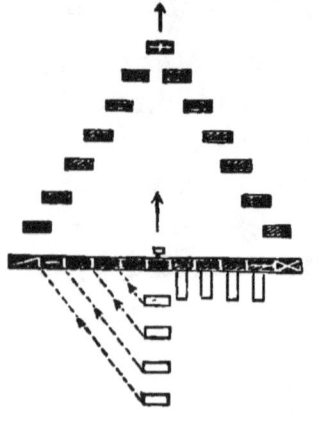 the First Vice Commander passing by the right to rear, commands: 1. *Files.* 2 *Right into echelon;* the Second Vice Commander stepping to the left of the column, commands: 1. *Files.* 2 *Left into echelon,* and both Vice-Commanders quickly go to the rear of their columns; the Senior Aid, without moving from his place, commands: 1. *Center files.* 2. *Mark time.*

At the command *march* the center column of files *marks time*, the leading files of the right and left column shorten the step. When these columns have passed about half their length the Senior Aid commands: 1. *Center column.* 2 *Forward.* 3 *Column right* 4. MARCH, which it executes; and the Senior Aid immediately commands: 1. *By the left flank.* 2. *Rear files.* 3. *Left front into line,* adding. 4 MARCH the instant before the Standard Bearer would have turned to the right

The Knights, who have changed direction to the right face to the left and advance in line by short steps; the rear files execute *left front into line,* the Senior Aid quickly takes his place on the right of his division; the Vice-Commanders form the last files of their respective divisions; the rear division, when formed, closes up on the other two with the full step, and the Commander commands: 1. *Forward* 2 MARCH. 3. *Guide center,* and places himself in front of the leading files, thus completing the triangle.

THE DISPLAY DRILL.

The triangle may be formed at open order (threes distance) if desired, by omitting the command for closing to half distance.

The center column may form the base of the triangle by wheeling around the standard, as before described for similar movement, if so instructed.

To Reduce Triangle.

1. *Column of threes.* 2. *Mark time.* 3. MARCH.

At the first command the Vice-Commanders command their respective divisions to *mark time*, the Senior Aid steps in front of his division, and commands, 1. *Right wing.* 2. *Left wheel*, and the Junior Aid facing the left wing of the second division, commands, 1. *Left wing.* 2. *To the rear.* 3. *Left wheel.* At the command *march* the first and third divisions and the Standard Bearer *mark time;* the half of the second division, which is at the right of the Standard Bearer, wheels to the left, describing a quarter circle about him; the left half of the division executes *to the rear, march,* and immediately commences the left wheel similar to the movement of the right wing. The Senior Aid commands, 1. *From right take distance by the right and left flanks*, and adds *march* the instant the wings have wheeled perpendicular to their late line, when both wings face toward the apex of the triangle, and, except the leading file, halts; the leading file marches forward and each Knight in succession resumes the forward march at the distance of fifty-four inches from the one in front.

Seeing that the head of the center column is nearly up to its place, the Commander commands. 1. *Form threes.* 2. MARCH. The Senior and Junior Aids quickly take their places on the right and left of the Standard Bearer, and Knights in the outer columns face and march directly to their places in column of threes; the Vice-Commanders take their posts at the head and rear of the column. The Commander commands *Forward* MARCH at the proper time.

Threes in Triangles.

Being in column of threes, at section distance.

1. *Threes in triangles.* 2. MARCH.

At the command *march*, given as the right foot strikes the ground, numbers one and three of each three *mark time* and numbers two take two short steps, and then all resume the full step.

If in column of threes at wheeling distance, it is executed as described, the leading three marching forward on the third step, and the others *halt;* each three in succession marching forward, at caution of its chief, when it has gained section distance from the three in its front.

The Vice-Commanders lead and follow the column at half distance (54 inches).

The Standard Guard forms triangle as other threes.

1. *Form threes.* 2. MARCH.

At *march*, the Knight forming the apex of each triangle marks time, the others advance by the short step, and the threes, united, march forward.

To Form Triangles from Column of Sections.

Being closed to half distance.

1. *Form triangle.* 2. *Threes half right and left.* 3. March.

At the second command the chief of third section commands *forward*, the right three of the leading section wheels on a movable pivot, *half right*, and upon completion of the wheel of one-eighth of a circle, each Knight faces to the late front, and by oblique steps, shoulders square to the front, close the apex of the triangle (to within twelve inches) with the left three, which executes the same movements to the left, and both *mark time;* the right and left threes of the second section wheel as described, advance obliquely, and unite in echelon with the threes of the first section, at the caution of their chiefs; the Vice Commanders take their places in echelon at the rear; the third section marches forward (breaking in the center sufficient to admit the Standard Bearer, who halts when the movement is commenced), and the Aids place themselves on the flanks at the base of the triangle. The Commander forms its apex in front.

The length of the steps and acuteness of the angles necessary will be seen and readily determined on once executing the movement.

If there are more than three sections, those in rear form a second triangle, a cross square, etc., as may be indicated by the commands and as they may have been before instructed.

Double sections may be formed into triangle by similar means, the commands being, 1. *Form triangle.* 2. *Sections right and left half wheel,* etc.

To Re-form Column of Sections.

1. *Form sections.* 2. March. 3. *Guide center.*

At the command march the First Vice Commander takes his place at the head of the column; the leading Knights take the short step while the others of the first section march forward to their places, and the section takes the thirty inch step; the threes of the second section march obliquely toward each other, unite, face to the front, re-form the sections as just described, and march forward when at section distance; the rear section marks time, until it gains its place in column, and marches forward; the Standard Bearer and other officers promptly take their proper places by the shortest line.

To Form Square From Column of Sections.
Being in march.
1. *Form square.* 2. MARCH. 3. *Forward.* 4. MARCH.

At the first command the chiefs of sections command as follows, viz.:

First section, *Mark time.* Second and third sections, 1. *Right and left forward* 2. *Files right and left.* Fourth section and Standard Guard, *Forward.*

At the second command the first section *marks time;* the right threes of the second and third sections execute the *right forward files right*, and close in column of files on the chief of first section and *mark time;* the left threes of the same sections execute the *left forward files*

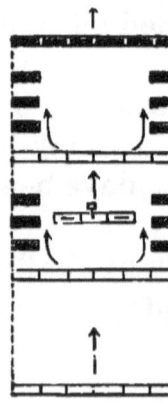

left, closing up and marking time in rear of the left guide of section one; the Standard Guard marches forward to the middle of the square, and the Commander gives the fourth command the instant the fourth section closes the square in rear.

The Commander and Vice-Commanders dart into the square as it is forming and form a line in front of the Standard Guard, the Commander on the right, the Second Vice-Commanders on the left; or, if so instructed, the Vice-Commanders may place themselves on the flanks of the first section, and the Aides place themselves on the flanks of the rear section (to increase the front); the sides of the square will oblique so as to cover the Vice Commanders instead of the chief and guide of the leading section; the Commander and standard only occupying the center, or the standard alone doing so.

Formation of square from double sections is similarly executed, and the officers, with the Standard Guard, form line, double rank, or triangle within the square Any odd sections in rear form as the Commander shall indicate by commands, thus: 1. *Form square.* 2. *Rear sections form triangle*, etc., and are formed and reduced as explained. This applies to nearly all the formations of like character.

To Reduce Square.

1. *Column of section.* 2. *Right and left front into line.* 3. March. 4. *Guide left.*

At the first command the First Vice-Commander, approaching near to the right side of the square, commands, in a low tone, *Left front into sections;* the Second Vice-Commander approaches near to the left side of the square and commands in a low tone, *Right front into sections;* the chief of the fourth section, *Mark time.* At the command *march* the first section moves forward; the second and third sections are re-formed as indicated by the commands, until each in succession has gained section distance, when, at command of their chiefs, they take the full step *forward*, and so with section four. The officers immediately resume their proper posts; the Standard Guard regulates its step so as to regain its place as soon as the second section advances.

To Reduce Greek Cross to the Left.

1. *Form column to the left.* 2. MARCH. 3. *Guide left.*
See page 134.

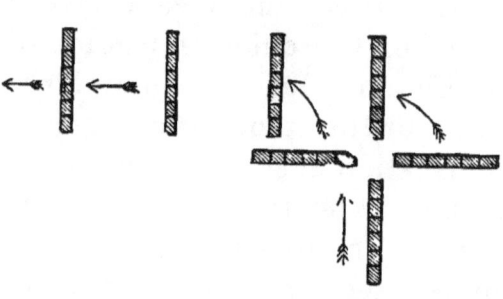

At the first command the First Vice-Commander orders: *First section by the left flank;* the chief of second section commands *left wheel;* the chief of the third section, and Second Vice-Commander cautions the third and fourth sections that they will have to *mark time.* The command *march* is given as the left foot strikes the ground, when the first section marches by the left flank; the second section wheels on a movable pivot to the left and follows the first. As the second section is about to pass in front of the third section its chief commands: 1. *Third section.* 2. *Left wheel.* 3. MARCH; when it wheels into its place in column. The Second Vice-Commander orders, 1. *Fourth section.* 2. *Forward.* 3. MARCH, and when it reaches the rear of the column, commands, 1. *By the left flank.* 2. MARCH.

To Form Square from Greek Cross.

1. *Form square.* 2. MARCH.

At the first command chiefs of double-sections (or sections) command:

1st and 4th double-sections—1. *By the left flank.* 2. *Right wheel*

2d and 3d double sections—*Left wheel.*

THE DISPLAY DRILL. 155

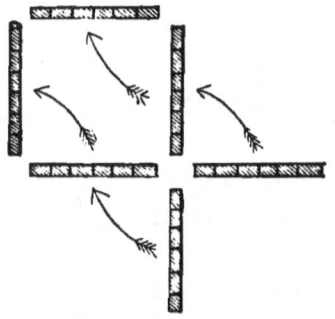
At the command *march* the double sections wheel as indicated by the commands; the double sections regulating their steps so that they will not interfere with others, and each completes its wheel as nearly as possible at the same instant. The Commander, and Vice Commanders place themselves within the square as before explained, and the Commander orders:

1. *By the right flank.* 2. *Square forward.* 3. MARCH. 4 *Guide center.*

The second and third divisions execute *by the right flank*, and with the rear subdivisions closed to their places the square, moves forward.

1. *Form column.* 2. MARCH. 3. *Guide left.*

At the second command chiefs of subdivisions see that their subdivisions gain their places in column by these movements. 1st, Subdivision—*Forward*, executed by shortening the steps a little. 2d, 1. *By the left flank.* 2. *Right wheel*, following in trace of the leading subdivision at subdivision distance.

3d and 4th Subdivisions—1. *Section.* 2. *Mark time.*

3d Subdivision executes, 1. *Forward* 2. *Column right.* 3. MARCH, and having gained its place in column. 1. *By the left flank.* 2. MARCH.

4th Subdivision. 1. *Forward.* 2. MARCH, when the 3d subdivision is at proper distance.

The Commander orders *Guide left* when the command *forward march* is given to the rear subdivision, and the full step is taken.

Or the cross may be reformed thus:

1. *Form Greek Cross.* 2. MARCH.

The subdivisions execute the following movements:

1st and 4th subdivisions—*Left wheel*, then *by the right flank.*

2d and 3d subdivisions—*Right wheel*, and seeing the movements completed the cross marches forward by the usual commands and means.

These hints are deemed sufficient for the execution of the movement.

To Form Star from Column of Threes (or Sections.)

1. *Form star.* 2. MARCH. 3 *Guide center.*

At the command *march* the First Vice-Commander places himself on the left of the leading three, which wheels in a circle about him, its pivot describing a circle of about forty eight inches in diameter, Commander places himself twelve inches in front and left of First Vice-Commander, half of whose body covers him (∵); the other threes advance and wheel on the same ground as the leading three, keeping the distance equal. As the rear three is about to commence the wheel the the Second Vice Commander quickly places himself by the side of the First Vice-Commander and the three officers form a triangle within the circling threes (∴).

The circular movement is kept up, in lieu of a direct march and innumerable radiations from, or formations about the center are made; for example:

1. *Threes right.* 2. MARCH.

Each three wheels and marches directly from the center.

1. *Threes right about.* 2. MARCH.

They execute the movement, and on nearing the center are caused to resume the former place in circular column, thus: 1. *Threes right.* 2. March. Then may follow: 1. *Form sections.* 2. *Left oblique.* 3. March; then 1. *Left threes.* 2. *To the rear.* 3. March causes those nearest the center to reverse the circle while the threes on the outer flank continue the march.

1. *To the rear.* 2. March.

Is executed by all. Then, after wheeling about the officers: 1. *Right threes.* 2. *To the rear.* 3. March; The third command is given as the threes of the original leading section approach, so that when executed all the sections will be re-formed.

The following may be executed consecutively:

1. *Right threes.* 2. *Full about.* 3. March.
1. *Left threes.* 2. *Full about.* 3 March.

The sections being united: 1. *Center forward.* 2. *Files left and right.* 3. March.

1. *Left files.* 2. *To the rear.* 3. March
1. *To the rear.* 2. March.

1. *Right files.* 2. *To the rear.* 3. March, in time to reform column of twos, as before. Then,

1. *Right and left front into sections.* 2 March.
1. *Sections in circle.* 2 *By the right flank.* 3 March.

At the third command each section executes by the right flank, march, and its leading file commences a circle (followed by the files of his section), whose diameter is about forty-eight inches, the files being careful to preserve their distances, and each head of section arriving at the same part of its own circle at the same time with the others.

THE DISPLAY DRILL.

1. *Column of files.* 2. *In circle.* 3. *Forward.* 4. MARCH.

At the command march, given as the leading file reaches the ground from which it commenced the last movement, it marches in a circle section distance about the officer following the trace of the one in front, and followed successively by the files of his section, as it unwinds, until all are marching in one circular column of files.

1 *Form threes.* 2. *Left oblique* 3. MARCH, forms column of threes marching in circle.

1. *Form sections.* 2. *Left oblique.* 3 MARCH re-forms sections.

1. *By the right flank.* 2 MARCH sends then off ray-like in columns from the center.

1. *To the rear.* 2. MARCH brings them back.

1. *By the right flank.* 2 MARCH, re-forms column of sections.

1. *Right by threes.* 2. MARCH, forms column of threes.

1. *Right by files.* 2. MARCH, forms column of files.

Now execute the following, giving each separate command as the feet successively strike the ground, commence by giving the first command as the left foot is planted:

1. *To the rear.* 2. MARCH. 3. *To the rear.* 4 MARCH. 5. *By the right flank.* 6. MARCH.

Thus execute to the rear march twice, then by the right flank. It requires practice, but when acquired is easily executed and is attractive. If desired, give fifth and sixth commands only. The files go off from the center independently and not together. They are returned by the command: 1. *To the rear.* 2. MARCH, and when the files approach each other:— 1. *By the right flank.* 2. MARCH re-forms circular column of files.

THE DISPLAY DRILL.   159

1. *Forward.* 2. MARCH.

At the second command the First Vice-Commander takes his place at the head and conducts the column straight forward, in a tangent, and the Second Vice-Commander places himself in rear as the column unwinds.

The foregoing are but suggestions. The combinations are without number. If there are eighteen in line t ey wheel in sections, etc , as before, forming obtuse angles; the Commander in the center. It looks quite as well or better with one in the center, but this can not be done so well if the Vice-Commanders are present. If the Standard is present it occupies the center.

During the march, in circular column of sections about the Commander, he may command: 1. *Threes.* 2. *Right forward.* 3. *Files right.* 4. MARCH, when each three executes it, forming two (circular) colums of files at forty-four inches interval. Then: 1. *Rear rest* 2. SWORDS, and march one of the colums *to the rear*, etc.

Or when in (circling) column of threes, or sections, command: 1. *To the rear.* 2. *Left* (or *right*) *wheel.* 3 MARCH when the subdivision execute the first and immediately commence the second movement.

School of the Battalion.

Uniformity and precision of movement, certainty as to the commands and the particular thing to be done, or that is required of the officers and commanderies, are essential in public parades and battalion movements.

A battalion of Knights of Honor is composed of two or more commanderies not exceeding eight, as a rule. In emergencies the number may be increased, but it is better for the commanderies to be consolidated and equalized, or formed as two or more battalions, under a Grand Commander.

Independent commanderies, of marked difference in numerical strength, with bands at irregular distances, detract very much from the beauty of the column that would result from a more systematic formation.

The first important thing is promptness. This can not be too strongly emphasized.

The details of this drill are given as full as the limit of space permits

In describing the movements, "at one" is sometimes used to indicate the first command: "at two" for the second command, and so on. Plain abbreviations are also used.

SCHOOL OF THE BATTALION. 161

Who Commands

When Commanderies appear in public, in their own State or out of it, they are under the immediate authority of the "Grand Commander," an officer upon whom under the constitution this duty devolves. But all are under the authority of the Grand Commander in whose jurisdiction they may at the time be

An officer properly in command *and present* may detail any Knight to assist in giving the oral commands, but he can not leave such Knight in charge when there are ranking officers present.

Battalion Officers.

The Colonel-Commander is chief of Battalion, and will be referred to in this work as the "Colonel."

The Battalion First Vice-Commander is second in rank, (corresponding to Lieutenant-Colonel) and will be referred to in this work as the "Battalion First Vice."

The Battalion Second Vice-Commander is third in rank, (corresponding to Major) and in this work will be referred to as "Battalion Second Vice."

These three officers are the *Field Officers*.

Staff Officers.

The *Adjutant* forms the battalion, does the writing at Headquarters, signs orders "By order of Colonel-Commander, A. B."

The *Battalion Orderly* assists the Adjutant (corresponding with the Sergeant-Major of the army); in this work he is referred to as "Orderly."

The Battalion Senior Aid commands the Standard or Color Guard. The Battalion Junior Aid is next in rank. The Standard, or Color Bearer, is a Knight, detailed on account of his steadiness in marching, correct carriage and physical strength and stature, to bear the principal standard or battalion colors. These three are called the Battalion Standard Guard, which may be increased in numbers as hereafter explained.

The Judge Advocate, Quartermaster and Commissary may form the rear (or in the front) rank of the Battalion Standard Guard as required.

When Commands are Repeated and Executed.

Officers in command of wings repeat commands whenever necessary; chiefs of commanderies repeat those, different from the others, which are to be immediately executed by their commanderies. In successive movemen's each chief of commandery gives the command necessary to insure the execution of the movement by his commandery at the proper time. Commands are executed on hearing them from the Colonel-Commander.

Rank and Position of Commanderies.

Commanderies take rank according to the dates of their several organizations, unless they voluntarily waive their proper rank.

They form in order of rank from right to left, and in battalion movements are designated, numerically, from right to left. when in line, and from front to rear when in column. as *first commandery, second commandery*, and so on

A SQUADRON is properly two mounted commanderies, but the nomenclature of the order forces the use of *division* (in U. S. infantry battalion drill, two companies) in the sense of a military platoon; hence we use *squadron* in this battalion drill, to indicate two commanderies, if more than two are present, whether mounted or on foot.

In column of squadrons commanderies are designated from the head of the column, and from right to left of each squadron, as, *first commandery; second commandery first squadron*, and so on

The numbers of commanderies and squadrons change when, by facing in the opposite direction, the left becomes the right of the line, and the rear the head of the column. If in passing from line into column, or the reverse, the designation is changed, they hold their last designation until the movement is completed, when the chiefs immediatly caution (such) *commandery*, so with the squadrons.

The ranking officer of the squadron commands it in column of squadrons, having regard to the rank of the officer himself, as well as his commandery (unless he waive his right).

For practice drill large commanderies can treat double-sections, or sections, as commanderies, placing the best drilled Knights in command.

Equalization of Commanderies.

In drill and parades it is often desirable that the Commanderies be numerically equal. Large commanderies may, for this purpose, be divided into two or more; one of which occupies its place according to rank, and the others on its left according to the direction of the commander. Small commanderies might be consolidated and take rank from the oldest commandery in the consolidation, according to the equities of the case. That is, if a senior commandery, taking the right, had one or more supernumeraries, it would not be just for these to be consolidated with the junior commandery so as to give it fictitious rank.

The Standards.

Unless every commandery has its standard and guard, those present could be grouped and form a Battalion Standard Guard, which occupies the center of the battalion. Its chief is the Battalion Senior Aide on its right, unless its number (always the multiple of three) exceeds six, when its chief may be detached, the same as a chief of commandery.

Its numerical strength never exceeds that of the commanderies. It would doubtless prove satisfactory for the Standard Bearer, as left file of the right center division of each commandery, to carry a light Guidon with the "Coat of Arms" of his commandery emblazoned upon it.

When chiefs of commanderies are referred to, the term applies as well, generally, to the chief of the Battalion Standard Guard.

Post of Officers.

The *Field Officers* are supposed to be mounted.

The Colonel-Commander is posted in front of the center of the line at a distance equal to about half its front, not exceeding thirty yards. He goes wherever his presence is necessary.

SCHOOL OF THE BATTALION. 165

The Battalion First and Second Vice-Commanders are on a line in front of the centers of the right and left wings, at a distance equal to about half the front of the wing.

* Col. Com.

* 2d B. Vice-C.   * 1st B. Vice-C.

Com's. Orderly * ——— * ——— * ——— * ——— † ——— * ——— * ——— * ——— * Adjt.

The Adjutant and Battalion Orderly, in maneuvers of the battalion, act as Adjutant and Sergeant Major respectively, and also as right and left general guides; they are posted on the right and left of the battalion, except when acting as Adjutant and Sergeant Major, when they are three yards from the flanks, and aid the Battalion Vice-Commanders.

Officers in charge of Commandery, and the chief of the Battalion Standard Guard, if he is not a part of the Guard itself, are two yards in front of the centers of their respective commands.

The Markers

Should, if practicable be Knights temporarily detached from the Battalion Standard Guard or flank commanderies, and their intervals left for them; otherwise they retire, after the line is formed, behind the flanks of the Battalion Standard Guard [abbreviated Bat. St. Gd.]; or in maneuvers, are one yard in rear of the right and left flanks of the battalion when it is in line; and the same distance from the leading and rear subdivisions on the opposite side from the guide, when in column.

SCHOOL OF THE BATTALION.

To Form the Battalion.

The commanderies form on their parade-grounds at the sound of the *assembly* [in army, at *adjutant's call*], and the Adjutant and Battalion Orderly, each covered by a marker, march to the battalion parade ground, when each posts a marker, facing the other, at a distance apart a little less than the front of a commandery; each standing three yards in rear of the marker nearest to him, the Adjutant being toward the right of the line. The Adjutant then takes a side step to the left the Battalion Orderly to the right, draw swords, face about, and each proceeds commandery distance toward the right and left of the line, when they halt and face about, and again cover the markers. The line is prolonged in the right wing by the First Vice-Commanders (as right guides), who precede their commanderies on the line by about fifteen yards and establish themselves facing the markers, each at commandery distance from the marker or Vice-Commander in front of him. The Adjutant assures the position of the right guides, placing himself in their rear (as before described) as they successively arrive. The line is similarly prolonged in the left wing by the Second Vice-Commanders as left guides; the Battalion Orderly assuring their position as they successively arrive.

The guides invert their swords in front of the center of the body, cross hilt above the chapeau, flat of the blade next to them.

The Bat. St. Gd. is the first established and is conducted by its chief, so as to arrive from the rear, parallel with the markers. When it arrives in rear of the line it is halted and its chief, placing himself facing to

SCHOOL OF THE BATTALION. 167

the front, near the left marker dresses the guard to the left—[or if there is no Bat St. Gd , then the right center commandery is so dressed by its chief], the breasts of the Knights opposite the markers, resting against their arms. The commanderies of the right wing form successively from left to right, each being halted three yards from the line and dressed to the left, as explained for the Bat. St. Gd The commanderies of the left wing form successively from right to left, and are dressed to the right In alignments the Vice-Commanders on the flank toward which the alignment is made, if not employed to mark the line, step back to enable the chiefs to align their commanderies.

Each chief commands: 1. (such) *Commandery* 2 *Support* 3. SWORDS, as soon as the chief next succeeding him in his own wing commands *front;* the flank commanderies *support swords* as soon as dressed.

THE BAND forms (at the place designated by the adjutant) at the sound of the *assembly of musicians* which precedes the *assembly*, and marches at the same time with the commanderies, playing in quick time, to its position in line

The Field Officers take their places, the Colonel-Commander only, facing the line

The Adjutant having assured the position of the First Vice-Commander of the right commandery, faces about, marches three yards to the right of the front rank, faces to the left, moves two yards to the front, halts and faces to the left; and when the last commandery arriving on the line is brought to *support swords*, commands: 1. *Guides*. 2 POSTS.

At this command the Orderly, chiefs of commanderies, passing through the intervals, made by the Vice-

Commanders and markers take their posts in line; the markers passing through the intervals made by the Vice-Commanders near them stepping one yard to the rear, who then resume their places; the Orderly takes his position on the left flank.

(The chief of Bat. St. Gd occupies the same relative position, if not forming a part of the guard itself, and is included when chief of commanderies are referred to.)

The Adjutant then passes along the front, in rear of the chiefs of commanderies, to the center, turns to the right, halts midway between the chiefs of commanderies and the Colonel-Commander, faces about, brings the battalion to a *carry* and a *present swords* (which the Colonel acknowledges by raising his chapeau), resumes his front, salutes the Colonel, and reports: *Sir the battalion is formed.*

The Colonel returns the salute with the right hand, directs the Adjutant to *take your post. Sir,* draws his sword, and commands: 1. CARRY. 2. SWORDS.

The Adjutant faces about, retraces his steps, and takes post on the right flank.

To Open Ranks.

Being at a halt.

1. *Rear open order.* 2. MARCH.

At the first command the Adjutant places himself three yards in rear of the right of the right flank, facing to the left; the Battalion Orderly places himself three yards in rear of the left of the left flank, faces to the right, and inverts his sword; the First Vice Commanders of the right, and Second-Vice-Commanders of the

SCHOOL OF THE BATTALION.

left commanderies, step back three yards opposite their places in line to mark the new alignment of the rear rank; they are aligned by the Adjutant on the Battalion Orderly.

At the command *march* the front rank dresses to the right and the rear rank steps to the rear, passes a little in rear of the established line, and dresses forward on the Vice-Commanders, who verify the alignment of their respective commanderies.

The chiefs of commanderies place themselves three yards in front of the center of their commanderies, dress to the right and cast their eyes to the front as soon as their alignment is verified.

The Colonel-Commander superintends the alignment of the commandery officers and front rank, and the Bat. First Vice the rear rank.

At the command *front*, the Bat. First Vice Commander and Bat. Second Vice-Commander take their places (p. 165); the Vice-Commanders place themselves on the line of the chiefs of commandery in front of the centers of the right and left wings of their commanderies; the Adjutant and Orderly step straight to the front and dress on a line of commandery officers; the Colonel-Commander, passing to the center in front of the line of commandery officers, places himself facing to the front, six yards in advance of the line of the Bat. First Vice-Commander and Bat. Second Vice-Commander.

To Close the Ranks.

1. *Close order.* 2. MARCH.

At the second command the officers face about and return to their places in line; the rear rank closes to facing distance.

To Open Order in Single Rank.

The same rules and commands apply except that numbers two or even numbers if sixes are counted, step to the rear, as before explained (School of the Commandery).

At the command, 1. *Close order.* 2. MARCH, the rear rank resumes its place in the front rank, and the movement is completed as before.

To Dismiss the Battalion.

Dismiss your commanderies. At this order each chief of commandery marches his commandery to its parade-ground, where it is dismissed.

To March in Line.

1. *Forward.* 2. *Guide center.* 3. MARCH.

At the second command the right and left general guides (Adjutant and Orderly) advance six yards to the front; the Battalion Standard Bearer (or Standard Bearer of the right center commandery if there be no Battalion Standard Guard) advances abreast of the Adjutant and Orderly, and the commander of the Battalion Standard Guard takes his place in the line. The chiefs of commanderies place themselves in the front rank on the right of their commanderies, and the First Vice-Commanders step back two yards straight to the rear; or, if there are two ranks, step back into the rear rank and cover their chiefs

The Bat. St. Gd. forms the basis for the alignment, its chief following in trace of the standard in its front. If there be no Bat. St. Gd. the right center commandery is the basis of the alignment. The chiefs of commanderies occasionally turn their heads slightly toward the basis of alignment (shoulders square to the front) in order to maintain themselves on the same line, each regaining his position, if lost, by almost insensible degrees

The Battalion First Vice-Commander and Battalion Second Vice-Commander place themselves in rear of the battalion, opposite their places in line, and superintend the march of the right and left wings, from the rear of their centers.

Similar rules govern the battalion movements as are prescribed for commanderies.

To Face the Battalion to the Rear and March it to the Rear.

Being in line.

1. *Threes right* (or *left*) *about.* 2. MARCH. 3. *Battalion.* 4. HALT. Or, 3. *Guide center.*

At one, the Battalion Standard Bearer and general guides, if not already there, return to their places in line; the battalion wheels about by threes at the second command. If halted, the chiefs of commanderies, placing themselves on the flanks of their commanderies toward the center, dress them in that direction; the Vice-Commanders on that flank step to the rear. In wheeling about by threes, when marching in line, each chief of commandery describes a semi-circle, whose radius is twenty-two inches, and thus places himself on the right or left flank of his commandery, according to his position before the movement.

If the march be continued, after wheeling about by threes, the Battalion Standard Bearer and general guides at the command *Guide center*, advance six yards in front of the line and assume the direction of the march; the chiefs of commanderies, if not already there, place themselves on the flanks of their commanderies farthest from the standard.

When a battalion in line wheels about by threes the Field Officers, unless otherwise directed, place themselves in rear by passing around its flanks. The battalion is then maneuvered by the same commands and means as when facing in the opposite direction.

To march the battalion a few yards to the rear, command:

1. *Battalion.* 2. About. 3. Face. 4. *Forward* 5. *Guide center.* 6. March.

Or, if in march, command:

1. *To the rear.* 2. March. 3. *Guide center.*

The officers retain their relative positions until it is again faced to the front.

To Oblique in Line and Resume the Forward.

1. *Right* (or *left*) *oblique.* 2. March.

Executed as before explained.

To resume the direct march: 1. *Forward.* 2. March.

To Halt the Battalion.

1. *Battalion.* 2. Halt.

If the direct march is not to be resumed.

1. *Standard and general guides.* 2. Posts.

The order is obeyed and chiefs of commanderies resume their places in front as the guides step into their intervals.

To Rectify an Alignment.

Commanders rectify the alignment.

At this command the chiefs of commanderies place themselves on the flanks of their commanderies toward the standard (the guides, or files, stepping to the rear) and successively dressing toward the center, when the preceding chief commands *front*. Each returning to his place in line after commanding *front*.

To Give General Alignment.

The Colonel-Commander places himself outside one flank of the battalion and commands:

1. *Standard and general guides on the line.* 2. *Guides on the line.* 3. *Center.* 4. DRESS. 5. *Standard and guides.* 6. POSTS.

At the first command the Battalion Standard Bearer and Adjutant and Orderly place themselves on the line and face to the Colonel-Commander, who establishes them by motion of the sword in the direction he wishes to give the battalion.

At two, the First Vice-Commanders of commanderies to the right of the Battalion Standard and Second Vice-Commanders of commanderies to its left, face toward the standard, and each places himself at commandery distance in rear of the one next before him, and aligns himself on the Battalion Standard Bearer and the General Guide beyond.

The chiefs of the commanderies hasten to place themselves on the flanks of their commanderies toward the standard, and the Vice-Commander on that flank quickly passes by the rear and occupies the interval left by the guide on the line.

The left file of Battalion Standard Guard places himself in the interval left by the Battalion Standard Bearer and the chief occupies the interval so made for him.

The Field Officers on the righ and left wings place themselves outside the General Guides and assure the position of the guides in there own wings.

At four, the commanderies move up in quick time against the guides, and each chief of commandery commands, 1. *Left* (or *right*). 2. Dress. 3. Front, according as he is on the right or left of the standard.

If the new line be oblique and at considerable distance from the battalion, the chiefs of commanderies conduct their commands so as to arrive parallel to their places in the line, then dress, as before explained.

At the sixth command the officers and guides resume their places in line. If the new direction of line be such that commanderies find themselves in advance, the Colonel before establishing guides, causes these commanderies to move to the rear.

To Change Direction in Line

1. *Battalion.* 2. *Right* (or *left*) *wheel.* 3. March.

At two, the Battalion Standard Guard and General Guides place themselves six yards in front, as before explained; the chiefs of commands place themselves on the flanks of their commanderies farthest from the Battalion Standard Guard; the field officer of the left wing places himself on the left of the left general guide, and the field officer of the right wing on the right of the front rank.

At the command *march* the chief of the right commandery stands fast, or halts, and is the pivot; the left general guide takes the full step, wheels as if on the marching flank; the chief of the left commandery follows in his trace, preserving distance; the Battalion Standard Bearer preserves his distance on the line with left general guide and pivot, or slightly in rear of it.

The field officers superintend the movements of the general guide and wing nearest them.

1. *Battalion* 2. HALT. Or, 1. *Forward*. 2. MARCH.
3. *Guide center*, is given when wheeled sufficiently.

At *forward* the Battalion Standard Bearer advances to the line of the general guides. At the second command resume the direct step; the field officers return to their posts.

To March by the Flank from Line.

1. *Threes right* (or *left*). 2. MARCH.

The Colonel-Commander marches on the side of the guide about thirty yards from the center of the column. The Bat. First Vice and Bat. Second Vice on the same side, about six yards from the head or rear of the column, each in his own wing, the Adjutant and Orderly between them and the column

In all movements on the march, from the order in line to the order in column, the Bat Standard Bearer, at the preparatory command, resumes his position in line.

The battalion may be faced to the right or left from line and marched forward, or marched by the flanks by the usual commands for a commandery.

To Break into Column of Threes from the Right or Left, to March to the Left or Right.

1. *Column of threes.* 2. *Break from the right* (or *left*) *to march to the left* (or *right*). 3. MARCH.

At *two*, the chief of the right commandery orders: 1. *Right forward.* 2. *Threes right.*

At the command *march*, repeated by the chief, the commandery moves in column of threes to the front; the chief commanding, 1. *Column left,* adding 2. MARCH 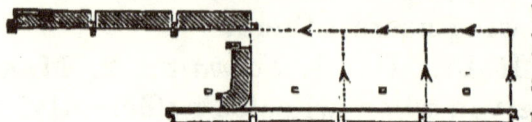 the instant the leading three has advanced commandery distance; the Vice-Commander then directs his march parallel with the front of the battalion. The chief of the second commandery orders, 1. *Right forward.* 2. *Threes right,* adding 3. MARCH when the leading guide of the first commandery arrives opposite his right three; the commandery advances and changes direction as explained for the first commandery, following in its rear.

The other commanderies successively conform to what is explained for the second.

Being in column of threes the battalion is halted, put in march, obliques, changes direction, marches to the rear, forms files, sections or divisions, etc., the same as a commandery, substituting *battalion* for *commandery.*

To Form Line to the Right or Left from Column of Threes.

1. *Threes right* (or *left*). 2. MARCH. 3. *Battalion.* 4 HALT.
Or, 3. *Guide center.*

The *halt* is given the instant the threes unite in line. Each chief of commandery places himself on the left of

SCHOOL OF THE BATTALION. 177

his commandery (the Vice-Commanders stepping back, as before explained), dresses his commandery to the left, commands *front*, and places himself in front of the center.

If the third command be for the guide (on completion of the wheel) the Bat. Standard and guides advance six yards in front of the line, and the chiefs place themselves on the flanks of their commanderies farthest from the standard, as before explained.

General Rules for Successive Formations.

That is, when several subdivisions arrive successively on the line.

In all such, except formation into line by two movements, the field officers at the head of the column or nearest the *point of rest* (where right of battalion is to rest if movement be to left, or where left will rest when movement is to right) establishes his two markers (facing point of rest) on the line opposite the right and left files of the subdivision first to arrive on the line. If formation be central, markers are placed on line in front of leading subdivisions, facing each other.

In all formations from halt, markers are established at preparatory command, indicating direction in which line is to extend; if marching, they hasten toward the point of rest and are established at command *march*. In formations on right (or left) in line, first marker is established subdivision distance to right (or left) of Head of column.

Formations front into line, they are established subdivision distance in front of head of the column.

Line is prolonged as explained in formation of battalion. When line is formed facing to rear, markers permit leading subdivisions to pass between, after which second marker closes to little less than commandery distance from the first; if formation be central, both markers close toward each other. Each guide so posts himself that his subdivision may cross line between him and guide next in front then closes to subdivision distance.

When the principles are well understood, markers may post themselves without aid of field officers, or Vice Commanders act when practicable

To Form Line on its Right or Left from Column of Threes.

1. *On right* (or *left*) *into line.* 2. MARCH.

From a halt. *At one*, repeated by chief of first commandery, the other chiefs of commanderies order: *forward.*

At *march*, repeated by the chiefs of commanderies, the leading commandery executes *on right into line;* the leading three arriving at three yards from the line, the chief halts the commandery and dresses it to the right against the markers. The other chiefs successively command, 1. *On right into line,* adding *march* when opposite the right of their places in line, halt their commanderies and dress them, as just explained.

If marching. the command to put the commanderies in motion is omitted.

To Form Line to the Front from Column of Threes.

1. *Right* (or *left*) *front into line.* 2. MARCH

From a halt. *At one.* chief of first commandery: 1. *Right front into line.* 2 *Double-time;* chief of second com-

SCHOOL OF THE BATTALION.

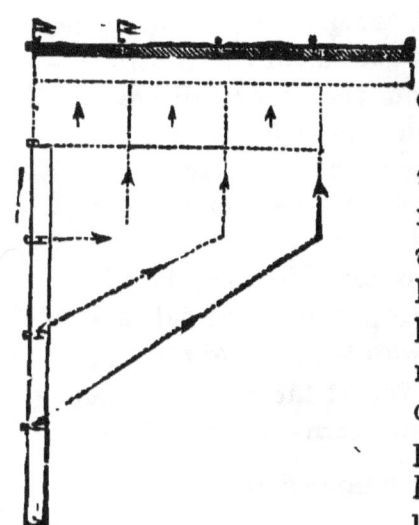

mandery: 1. *Forward.* 2. *Column right;* chiefs of other commanderies: 1. *Forward.* 2. *Column half right.* At *march*, repeated, first commandery executes *right front into line* in double time; is halted at three yards from line and dressed against markers. Chief of second commandery conducts it opposite the left of its place in line, changes direction to the left, and chief commands: 1. *Right front into line.* 2. *Double time*, adding 3. MARCH, when at commandery distance from line, places himself in front of its center, and when at three yards from the line, halts the commandery and dresses it to the left. The other chiefs conduct their commanderies to a point twice commandery distance in rear of the left of their places in line, change direction half left, and when at commandery distance from the line, conform to what has been explained for the second commandery.

If marching omit the command *forward.*

To Form Line to the Front, Faced to Rear, from Column of Threes.

1. *Right* (or *left*) *front into line, faced to rear.* 2. MARCH.

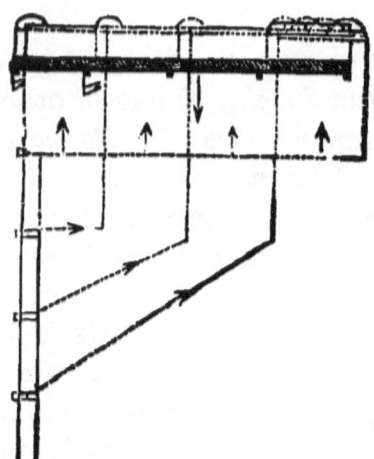

Executed as before explained, except commanderies are not halted till three yards beyond the line; where the commanderies at command of their chiefs execute *threes left about*, halt and dress to the right

In forming line, faced to rear, threes wheel about toward the *point of rest.*

To Form Line by Two Movements from column of Threes.

A part of the column having changed direction to the right.

1. *Threes left.* 2. *Rear commanderies left front into line.*
3. MARCH.

Chiefs whose commanderies have changed direction, repeat one and three, halt their commanderies as threes unite in line, then dress to right, remaining on line till *Guides,* POST.

March is given as head of a commandery is about to change direction. Rear commanderies execute *left front into line*

To form line faced to rear. Column having changed direction as before, 1. *Threes right.* 2. *Rear commanderies left front into line faced to rear.* 3. MARCH.

This and like formations to the left are executed similar to those explained.

SCHOOL OF THE BATTALION. 181

To Form Column of Sections from Line.

1. *Center forward.* 2. *Threes left and right.* 3. MARCH.
4 *Guide (right or left).*

At *two*, chief of right center commander orders:
1. *Left forward.* 2. *Threes left.* Chief of left center commandery orders: 1 *Right forward.* 2. *Threes right.* Other chiefs: *Threes left* (or *right*), according as they are in the right or left wing.

At *march*, repeated, column of sections is formed. The Colonel-Commander marches at twelve yards from center of column on the side of the guide. The field officers of each wing six yards from flank of the column, abreast of his leading guide; Adjutant and Orderly abreast of the guides in rear of the column.

[The Bat St Gd may lead this movement, if present.]

To Form Line from Column of Sections.

1. *Right and left front into line.* 2. MARCH.

Executed by each wing, as before explained. The markers are established for the Bat. St. Gd. [or right center commandery, if there be no Bat St. Gd]

To Form Line to the Right or Left from Column of Sections.

1. *Threes right* (or *left*). 2. *Left* (or *right*) *commanderies on right* (or *left*) *into line* 3. MARCH

The chiefs of right commanderies repeat the first and third commands, halt their commanderies as they unite in line, dress them to the left and remain on the left until the command *guides, posts* The Bat. St. Gd. and commanderies of the left wing execute *on right into line*. The field officer of left wing assures position of guides of the left commanderies.

182   SCHOOL OF THE BATTALION.

To form Column of Commanderies from Line.

1. *Commanderies right* (or *left*) *wheel.* 2. MARCH.

At one, the chiefs of commanderies repeat *right wheel.* At *march* each commandery wheels as before explained, each chief halting and dressing his commandery to the left.

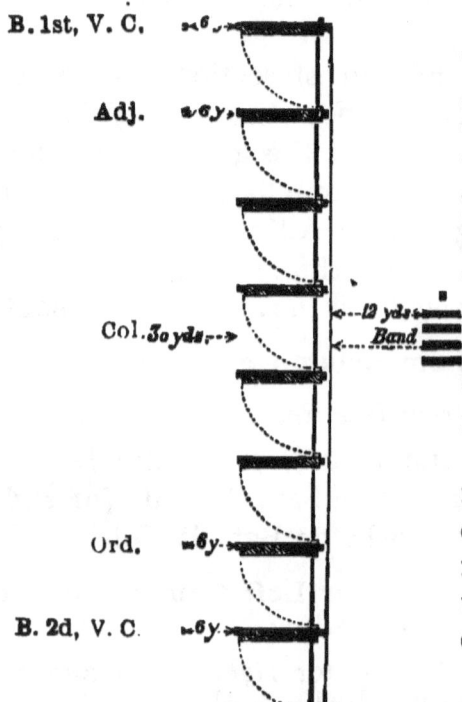

The chiefs having commanded *front,* the guides, although some of them may not be in the direction of the preceding guides, stand fast, in order that the error may not be extended through the column; the guides not in direction come into it in march.

The band is on the flank, as shown in the cut, in the drill; or may march at the head of the column if so directed.

If the battalion be in march, at the first command, the chiefs of commanderies place themselves before the centers thereof; at *march* pivots halt and then turn gradually in their places; the wheel is completed as from a halt

In column the field officers and general guides take

SCHOOL OF THE BATTALION. 183

their places, as shown in the plate, and change to the designated flank when the guide is changed. [So band changes if not at head of column].

To Form Column from Line and Move Forward without Halting.

1. *Continue the march.* 2. *Commanderiès right* (or *left*) *wheel.* 3. MARCH. 4. *Forward.* 5. MARCH. 6. *Guide* (*left* or *right*).

Wheel as before; chiefs remain in front of centers. At fifth command march forward, or in the direction the field officer at head of column indicates for leading guide, and others follow in his trace, preserving distance

The battalion breaks into column of squadrons, etc., in the same manner, substituting *squadrons* for *commanderies*. The chief of squadron performs the same duties as chief of commandery, the Junior chief places himself in the interval between the two commanderies, if not already there. The guide on the right or left of the squadron is its guide.

In wheel by squadron, if there be an odd commandery, its chief commands: 1. *Forward.* 2. *Guide right* (or *left*), according as the wheel is to the right or left, repeats the command *March*, adding 1. *Right* (or *left*) *wheel* in time to add 2. MARCH when the commandery has advanced commandery distance, when it wheels on a fixed pivot, is halted and dressed as before explained.

To Form Column of Commanderies to the Rear from Line.

1. *Right of commanderies rear into column.* 2. *Threes right.* 3. MARCH.

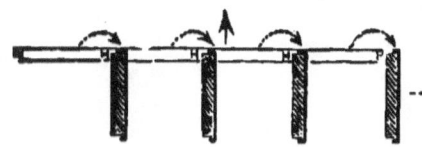

Being at halt. At the first command each chief places himself four feet in front of the right file of his commandery facing to the right; at *threes right* cautions the right three to wheel to the right about. The movement is executed as in divisions

Squadrons are formed in column to the rear by similar commands and means.

To Break from the Right or Left, to March to the Left or Right from Line.

1. *Commanderies break from the right* (or *left*) *to march to the left* (or *right*). 2. MARCH.

Being at a halt.

At one, the chief of the first commander orders, 1. *Forward*. 2. *Guide left*. At *march*, repeated by its chief, the right commandery moves forward, the chief commanding, 1. *Left turn*, adding 2 MARCH when the

guide has advanced commandery distance; the left guide then marches on a line parallel with the front of the battalion. The second commandery executes the movement by the same commands and means; its chief putting it in march when the first commandery arrives opposite its left; the guide, after turning, follows in trace of the left guide of the first. The others successively execute the same movement. Don't lose distance.

To March Column Forward, Halt it, Face it to the Rear, etc.

Executed by commands and means similar to like movements of a commandery

To Change Direction in Column.

1. *Column right* (or *left*). 2. MARCH.

Being in march. At the first command a marker (if markers are used) places himself abreast of the guide, on the left of the leading subdivision. The chief of this subdivision commands: *Right wheel*, repeats the MARCH, and on completion of the wheel, commands:

1. *Forward.* 2. MARCH.

The marker, at the command *march* by the Colonel-Commander, halts and faces to the column, remains un-

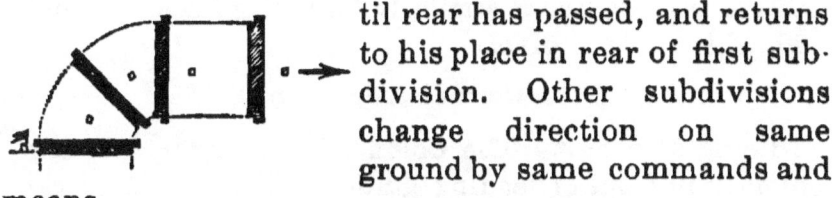

til rear has passed, and returns to his place in rear of first subdivision. Other subdivisions change direction on same ground by same commands and means.

To Put Column in March and Change its Direction at the Same Time.

1. *Forward.* 2. *Guide* (*left* or *right*). 3. *Column right* (or *left*). 4. MARCH. Or, 3. *Column half right*, etc.

To Form Line to the Left or Right from Column.

1 *Left* (or *right*) *into line wheel.* 2. MARCH. 3. *Guides.* 4. POSTS.

Being at a halt. At the first command chiefs of commanderies caution *left wheel;* the right guide of the leading commandery places himself facing the leading guide of the column at nearly commandery distance in front of him, so as to be opposite one of the right files of the commandery when the wheel is completed; the guide is assured in his position by field officer at head of the column.

At *march* the commanderies wheel to the left on fixed pivots. Each chief of commandery faces his command to observe the wheel; moves toward the point where its marching flank is to rest, and when it is near the line commands: 1. *Commandery.* 2. HALT. At *halt* the chief of commandery places himself on the line, by the side of the left file of the commandery next on the right, then commands, 1. *Right.* 2. DRESS. 3. FRONT. At *dress* the commandery dresses up between its chief and its left file; the file of the right commandery, who finds himself opposite its right guide, rests his breast lightly against the left arm of their guide.

If marching, line is similarly formed, guides halt, and wheel is on fixed pivot.

To Correct Alignment.

Being at a halt. The Colonel Commander, placing himself in front of leading guide, and facing him, establishes himself and guide next in rear, then commands:

1. *Right* (or *left*) *guides.* 2. COVER.

Right guides exactly cover those in front at subdivision distance; field officers in front and rear of column facing guides assist.

1. *Right* (or *left*). 2. DRESS.

Chiefs repeat, align their subdivisions and command, FRONT If a commandery is out of place, its chief gives necessary preparatory command (*forward, backward* or *side step*) adding *march* at command *dress* by Colonel-Commander. When it approaches guide, chief halts and dresses it up to the guide.

To Form Line and Move Forward.

1. *Continue the march.* 2. *Left* (or *right*) *into line wheel.* 3. March. 4. *Forward.* 5. March. 6. *Guide center.*

Wheel on fixed pivots, which mark time as explained; guide remains on flank of leading commandery. At the sixth command standard and general guides step six yards to front of line, and chief of commandery places himself in front rank, as before explained.

Column of Squadrons is formed in line similarly; the chiefs of squadrons command, 1. *Right.* 2. Dress, then (to commandery on his left), 1. (such) *commandery.* 2. Front; the chief of junior commandery, 1. (such) *commandery.* 2. Front (to commandery on his left). Odd commandery moves up to commandery distance, its guide covering guide in front, if not there.

Practice these without equalizing commanderies; put column in march; commanderies gain trace and distance of guides by obliques at command of chiefs. Colonel-Commander assists to gain distance by causing column to *mark time* or take *short step;* those not at proper distance, or alignment, gain it.

To Form Column on Right or Left.

Being in march, change guide, if not there, to flank toward which movement is to be made.

1. *On right* (or *left*) *into line.* 2. March.

At one, chief of first commandery commands. *Right turn* and repeats *march;* arriving at three yards from markers, chief halts and dresses it to the right. The

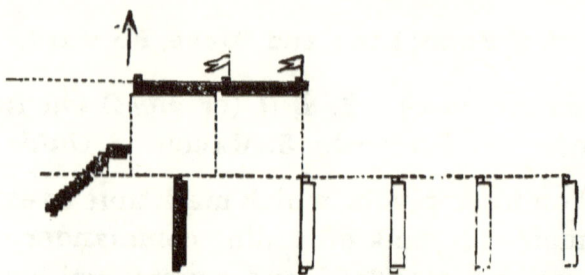

other commanderies continue the march, each chief giving command, *Right turn*, adding 2. MARCH upon arriving opposite the right of its place in line, and are halted and dressed as explained for first commandery.

To Form Line to the Front from a Halt.

1. *Right* (or *left*) *front into line.* 2 *Commanderies right* (or *left*) *half wheel.* 3. MARCH, 4. *Forward.* 5. MARCH. 6 *Guide left* (or *right*

At one, chief of first commandery, 1. *Forward.* 2. *Guide left;* at second command all other chief of com‑

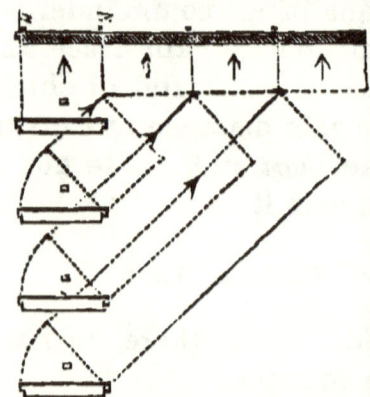

manderies caution *right half wheel;* at third command, repeated by chiefs, the first commandery advances, and when three yards from line, is halted and dressed to left against markers: the other commanderies wheel half right on fixed pivot, chiefs repeating fourth, fifth and sixth commands. At fifth command, given the instant the eighth of circle is completed, they cease to wheel and march forward. At sixth command the left guides of commanderies march directly to their front.

SCHOOL OF THE BATTALION.   189

The left of second commandery arriving nearly opposite the right of the first its chief commands, 1 *Left half turn.* 2. MARCH, the instant the left of company is opposite its place in line; and its chief commands 1. *Commandery*, adding 2. HALT at three yards from the line, then dresses his commandery.

When left of third commandery arrives opposite right of the second it turns half left, is halted and dressed as just prescribed, and other commanderies execute successively what is prescribed for the third.

In march the movement is similarly executed, the leading commandery approaches markers with guide toward point of rest, at command of chief of commandery, if necessary, at preparatory command.

To Form Line to the Front Faced to rear from Column.

Executed as before, except commanderies march three yards beyond the line; wheel about by threes, halt, and are dressed toward the point of rest.

To Form Column of Commanderies into Line by two Movements.

Part of column having changed direction to the right,

1. *Left into line wheel.* 2 *Rear commanderies left front into line.* 3. MARCH.

At one, chiefs of commanderies that have changed direction, caution *left wheel.* At second command chief of each commandery that has not changed direction except leading one, commands, *Left half wheel.* At *march*, repeated by chiefs of rear commanderies, those which have changed direction to right execute *left into line wheel*, rear commanderies *left front into line* as before described, the chiefs of rear commanderies upon completing the half wheel, adding 1. *Forward.* 2. MARCH. 3. *Guide right.*

Column having partly changed direction to the left, line is formed by similar commands and means.

To Advance by Flank of Subdivisions from Line.

1. *Commanderies* (or *squadrons*). 2. *Right* (or *left*) *forward.* 8. *Threes right* (or *left*). 4. MARCH. 5. *Guide* (*right, left* or *center*).

Each commandery (or squadron) executes *right forward threes right.* The Colonel-Commander marches abreast of chiefs of leading subdivisions, twelve yards from flank, on the side of guide: or if guide be center, then on either flank, other field officers six yards outside of column abreast of chiefs of subdivisions; they are covered by Adjutant and Orderly, who march abreast of rear guides.

To Form Line from Subdivisions when Marching by the Flank of Subdivisions.

1. *Commanderies* (or *squadrons*). 2. *Left* (or *right*) *front into line.* 3. MARCH. 4. *Battalion.* 5. HALT.

Each commandery (or squadron) executes the second command at the command *halt;* and is dressed to the right

If executed in double time the Colonel-Commander commands: *Guide center,* immediately after the command MARCH; the standard and General Guides ad-

SCHOOL OF THE BATTALION. 191

vance six yards in front of line, and chiefs of commanderies place themselves on the flanks of their commanderies farthest from the Bat. St. Gd. the guides on that flank stepping back, as before explained, except the guides on the flank commanderies of the battalion.

To Form Column of Subdivisions when Marching by the Flank of Subdivisions (and the Reverse).

1. *Threes right* (or *left*). 2 MARCH. 3. *Guide* (*right* or *left*), etc.

To March by the Flank of Subdivisions from Column of Threes, etc.

1. *Commanderies* (or *squadrons*, etc). 2. *Column right* (or *left*). 3. MARCH. 4. *Guide* (*right, left* or *center*).

The same command, omitting the fourth, reforms column of threes; each chief of commandery goes to the head of his commandery; the squadrons unite in column of threes.

To Form Column of Threes from Column of Commanderies and Squadrons and to Form again in Column.

1. *Commanderies* (or *squadrons*) 2 *Left* (or *right*) *forward*. 3 *Threes right* (or *left*). 4. MARCH.

To form again in column

1. *Commanderies* (or *squadrons*). 2. *Left* (or *right*) *front into line*. 3. MARCH. 4 *Battalion*. 5. HALT.
Or 4 *Guide left* (or *right*).

The subdivisions execute these movements simultaneously. Or these movements may be executed by commanderies successively, if so ordered, by designating them. They may also be executed in like manner by any subdivision of battalion.

To Close Column to Half Distance.

Being at a halt.

1. *Close column to half distance.* 2. *Forward.* 3. MARCH. 4 *Guide left* (or *right*).

At two, the chief of the leading squadron (or commandery) commands, 1. *First squadron* (or *commandery*). 2. *Stand fast.* The other squadrons march forward and are successively halted and dressed to the left by their chiefs when they arrive at commandery (or division) distance.

To Deploy Column.

See Display Drill. It is similarly executed.

To Form Line to the Right or Left from Column of Squadrons, etc., at Half Distance.

1. *Right* (or *left*) *into line wheel.* 2. *Left* (or *right*) *commanderies on right* (or *left*) *into line.* 3. MARCH.

At one, the chiefs of right commanderies caution, 1. (Such) *commandery.* 2. *Right wheel,* the left guide of the

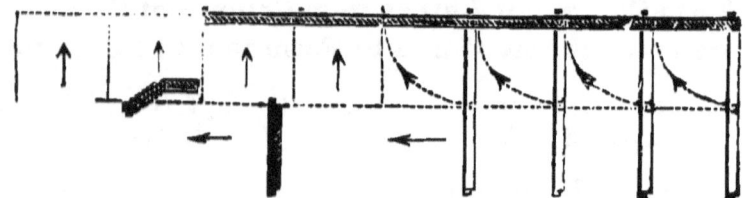

leading right commandery places himself on the line of the right guides, facing them, and so as to be opposite one of the three files on the left of his commandery; chief of left commanderies: 1. *Forward.* 2. *Guide right.* At *march,* repeated by chiefs, the right commanderies wheel into line to the right; the left commanderies move forward, and when the leading one is opposite its place, executes *right turn*. The field officer of the left wing assures the positions of the guides of the left commanderies.

If marching, the Colonel-Commander orders guide on flank toward which movement is to be made, if not there, and chiefs of left commanderies omit the *forward march*.

To Form Column of Commanderies from Column of Squadrons, and the reverse.

1. *Right* (or *left*), *by commanderies*. 2. March. 3. *Guide left* (or *right*).

Being at a halt. At the first command chiefs of right commanderies: *Forward*. Chiefs of left commanderies: *Right oblique*. At *march*, repeated by chiefs, right commanderies move forward, chiefs repeating command for guide; the chiefs of left commanderies command MARCH the instant their commanderies are disengaged, at which they oblique to right, regulating step to maintain distance. When they are in rear of right commanderies thier chiefs command, 1. *Forward*. 2. March. 3. *Guide left;* the second command is given the instant the left guide arrives in trace of the left guide of the right commandery.

1. *Form squadrons left* (or *right*) *oblique*. 2. March. 3. *Battalion*. 4. Halt.

Being in column of commanderies.

At one, chief of right commandery of each squadron: 1. *Forward*. 2. *Guide left;* chief of the left commandery: *Left oblique*. At *march*, repeated by the chiefs, leading commanderies move forward; rear commanderies oblique to left. The fourth command, repeated by chiefs of leading commanderies, is given when they have advanced commandery distance; each chief dresses his commandery, being careful that guides cover, and places himself in front of its center.

To Change Front of Battalion.

1. *Change front on first* (or *eighth*) *commandery.* 2. *Commanderies right* (or *left*) *half wheel.* 3. MARCH. 4. *Forward.* 5. MARCH. 6. *Guide right* (or *left*).

At one, chiefs, if not there, place themselves in front of centers of their commanderies.

At two—chief of right commandery: *Right wheel;* other chiefs caution *right half wheel.* At *march,* repeated by chiefs, right commandery right wheels on fixed pivot, and its chief commands, 1. *Forward.* 2. MARCH. 3 *Guide right*, and having arrived at three yards from the line, its chief halts it and dresses it to right against the markers.

The other commanderies make half wheels to right on fixed pivots, and movement is completed similar to left front into line from column of commanderies. The chiefs of rear commanderies command 1. *Right half turn,* adding, 2. MARCH, when their right guides are opposite their places in line. (See cut).

Oblique change of front on first (or *eighth*) *commandery,* is similarly executed.

Change of front on right or left commandery and face to rear is executed by adding *faced to rear,* to the first command, and similar to front into line faced to rear from column of commanderies.

 Dress Parade.

The battalion is formed as before **explained**; [or if it be of but one commandery, its divisions are officered and are treated as commanderies, the Commander acting as Colonel-Commander].

The Colonel-Commander takes his post at a convenient distance in front of the center, facing the line (generally a distance equal to about one-half its front) and stands with arms folded until just before the command to *present*, when he comes to *attention*.

The Adjutant having commanded *guides*, *posts*, directs the first Commander to bring his commandery to *parade rest*. Each Commander in succession, commencing on the right, faces about and commands:

1. (Such) *Commandery*. 2. *Carry*. 3. SWORDS. 4. *Parade*. 5. REST, and returns to his place.

The Adjutant then commands, SOUND OFF, and takes the position of *parade rest*. The band, commencing to play in common time, marches six yards to the front, then to the left past the left of the line, and back over the same ground to its place, playing in quick time, giving a flourish before starting, after the countermarch at the left, and on its return to the right.

The Adjutant steps two yards to the front faces to the left and commands:

1. *Battalion.* 2. ATTENTION. 3. *Carry.* 4. SWORDS. 5. *Rear open order.*

Aligns the guides of the rear rank, again comes to the front, and commands: 6. MARCH, verifies the alignments, commands, 7. FRONT, and passes in rear of the line of Commanders to the center, turns to the right, marches to a point midway between the Colonel-Commander and the line occupied by the commanders, faces about, and commands:

1. *Present.* 2. SWORDS.

To this the Colonel Commander raises his chapeau in acknowledgment. The Adjutant then faces about, salutes the Colonel-Commander, and says:

Sir, the parade is formed.

The Colonel-Commander, saluting with the hand:

Take your post, Knight.

The Adjutant takes post three yards to the left and one yard to the rear of the Colonel-Commander passing by his right and rear. The Colonel-Commander now draws his sword, commands, *Carry,* SWORDS, and exercises the battalion in the manual, concluding with, *Order,* SWORDS He directs the Adjutant to *Receive the reports,* and return his swords.

The Adjutant retraces his steps to the point at which he saluted the Colonel-Commander, and commands:

1. * *Secretarys to front and center.* 2 MARCH.

---

* *First Vice-Commanders* may be substituted for *Secretaries* if desired.

At the first command the secretaries come to a *carry;* at the second they step two yards to the front and face to the center; the drum-major also steps two yards forward, and faces to the left At *march,* they close on the center in front of and between the Standard and Adjutant, two yards from the former, and successively face to the front. The Adjutant then commands, REPORT. At this command the drum-major* and Secretaries (or First Vice-Commanders), commencing on the right, successively salute and report, *Band present or accounted for,* or (so many) *absent* The Secretaries (or First Vice Commanders) report (such) *Commandery No — present or accounted for,* or give the number present and the number absent. When completed, the Adjutant commands:

1. *Secretaries* (or *First Vice Commanders.* 2. *Outward.* 3. FACE. 4 *To your posts.* 5. MARCH.

Then they all retrace their steps and resume *order arms.*

The Adjutant faces about, salutes, and says, *Sir, all present, or accounted for;* or he reports the number absent.

The Colonel-Commander acknowledges the salute and says, *Publish the orders, Knight.* The Adjutant, facing the battalion says:

Attention to orders,

Returns his sword and reads the orders.† After which he draws his sword, faces about, salutes the Colonel-Commander, and reports:

---
*The d um-major, before making his report, salutes by bringing his staff to a vertical position, the head of the staff up and opposite the left shoulder.

†If he has sword knot he drops sword.

Sir, the orders are published.

The Colonel-Commander acknowledges the salute, and commands:

*To your devotions, Knights.**

The Adjutant returns to his place at the rear and right of the Colonel-Commander who commands:

1. *Battalion.* 2. Un-cover.

They *uncover*, and the Prelate faces parallel to the front, and repeats the Lord's Prayer, all joining in it, or short extemporaneous prayer. After a pause the Colonel-Commander *re-covers* and commands, 1. *Battalion.* 2. Re-cover. The Prelate faces to the front, and the Colonel-Commander directs the Adjutant to

Dismiss parade, Knight.

At which the Adjutant returns to his place, as before, and commands:

Parade is dismissed.

The Commanders, and Vice-Commanders now return their swords, face to the center, step off at the same time with the Adjutant, close upon the center, and successively face to the front. The two nearest the center preserve an interval for the Adjutant, who passes through, one yard to the rear, halts, faces about steps into his place, and commands:

1. *Forward.* 2. *Guide center.* 3. March.

The bands plays and when within five yards of the Colonel Commander, the Adjutant commands:

---

*This part may be omitted if desired.

DRESS PARADE.

1. *Officers.* 2. HALT.

At the second command the officers halt and salute with the band, the music ceases; the hands remain at the visor, till the salute is acknowledged, and drop at the same time with the Colonel Commander's hand, who gives such instruction as he desires, which concludes the ceremony, and the officers disperse; the band plays, the First Vice Commanders return to their commanderies (or the Senior Aid may take charge if so directed), and command:

1. *Carry.* 2. SWORDS. 3. *Close order.* 4. MARCH.

The First Vice-Commanders (or Senior Aids) march the commanderies to their quarters and dismiss them, as they may previously have been instructed.

It would add much to the display if, after the parade is dismissed, the commanderies should march off in echelon, commandery front, beginning on the right; the second commandery starting when the first has marched commandery distance, or half commandery distance.

Review.

Reviewing officer takes post in front of the center of battalion, the point being indicated by a marker or standard previously established. The Adjutant also posts markers at points where the column will have to change direction in order that the right flank, in passing, shall be at six or eight yards from the reviewing officer, whose staff, or other grand officers, are six yards in his rear.

The officer in command, being in front of and facing the center commands:

1. *Prepare for review.* 2. *Rear open order.* 3. MARCH. 4. FRONT.

At the command *march* the ranks are opened and the lines are dressed as before explained.

Officer in command, seeing the ranks aligned, returns to the right of the line of chiefs of commanderies, faces to the left, commands FRONT, and passing to the front of this line of officers places himself six yards in front of the line of field officers, opposite the center and facing to the front. The reviewing officer now approaches a few yards and halts, when the officer in command faces about and commands:

1. *Present.* 2. SWORDS.

The officers, standards, and Knights *present*, and if the reviewing officer be the grand officer, the band plays a march or trumpets flourish, according to his rank. Officer in command faces about and salutes with the sword. The reviewing officer acknowledges the salute by raising his chapeau, the band ceases to play, and the officer in command again faces the line and commands:

1. *Carry.* 2. SWORDS.

He joins the reviewing officer, who proceeds to the right of the band, and passing to the left in front of the line of chiefs of commanderies, returns in rear of the rear rank, the band playing until he leaves the right to return to his station.

The officer in command now returns to his post in front of the center and command:

1. *Close order.* 2. MARCH.

Which having been executed, he adds:

1. *Commanderies (divisions or sections), right wheel.* 2. MARCH.

At the second command the commanderies break into column of commanderies (divisions or sections).

The band wheels and marches so that its rear rank will be nine yards in advance of the leading chief of commandery. The Battalion Vice Commanders, Adjutant and Orderly on the left of the column.

The officer in command now commands:

1. *Pass in review.* 2. *Forward* 3 *Guide right.* 4 MARCH.

The band plays; the column advances and changes direction to the left, and again to the left at points indicated, so as to pass about six yards in front of the reviewing officer, and without command from the officer in command, who takes his place three yards in advance of the chief of the leading commandery (or officer in command of the leading subdivision), after the second change of direction. The band, having passed the reviewing officer, wheels to the left out of column, takes post in front and facing him, where i remains till the rear of the column has passed, when it coun er marches to the rear and returns to its place before the review, ceasing to play when the column approaches its original position If there is more than one commandery (not in battalion formation) each band ceases to play when the rear of its commandery has passed the reviewing officer, and follows in its rear until its commandery is halted, when it passes by the rear to its place on the right.

When the column is passing in review, the officers and standards *salute*, each commencing six yards from the reviewing officer, and resuming the carry when six yards past; the Knights in line retain the *carry*.

If the reviewing officer be entitled to it, the trumpets flourish, etc , and the band continues to play.

The drum major, marching in review, passes the staff between the right arm and the body, the head to the front, and salutes with the left hand

In saluting. all the officers turn the head and look toward the reviewing officer, who acknowledges only the salutes of the officer in command and the standards.

The officer in command having saluted, places himself, if mounted, on the right of the reviewing officer, and there remains until his battalion has passsed, when he rejoins the battalion. The head of the column having executed a second change of direction to the left, after passing the reviewing officer, the officer in command commands, *guide left*, and when it arrives on its original ground, wheels it into line, ranks are opened and swords are presented as before; this being acknowledged, terminates the review.

General Parade.

General Parades are unfortunately often marred by some one, who seems to have little regard for well devised plans.

It requires very little individual effort to conform to rules, and their general observance would add materially to the pleasure at general gatherings.

On such occasions the observance of the following rules is important.

GENERAL HEADQUARTERS should be established; its chief and staff prepared at all hours to furnish information concerning existing orders; localities of grand or subordinate commanderies; assignment of quarters for new arrivals; a post office for mailing or distributing letters to individuals (or commanderies), etc.; rosters, alphabetically or systematically arranged, so as to be of some use. In short, a place where any reasonable demand for information would be met with courteous and intelligent response.

HEADQUARTERS for every organized battalion and commandery present, and at least an intelligent servant left in charge, who could receive and properly deliver messages, letters, or orders left in absence of the Knights.

GENERAL PARADE

To INSURE ALL THIS, Commanders should report their arrivals at General or Battalion Commandery Headquarters, and leave a duplicate list of the Knights of their command, including the ladies and band accompanying it; at their own headquarters to keep a register of the locality of the private quarters of each individual. At stated hours every Knight should report at his commandery headquarters, in order that all may feel some confidence in expecting to find their friends there at that time; or general or special information concerning the parade, which should be given at roll call.

The Battalion Commanders should report at general headquarters immediately on their arrival.

Orders should be promptly sent to Battalion Commanders, who should require a staff officer to promptly deliver them to subordinate commanders. Disobedience of lawful orders ought to be followed with prompt and effectual discipline. Delay blunts the point of discipline.

Nothing wearies men in ranks so much as unnecessary waiting and vexatious halts. This is demoralizing to an army, therefore *promptness is the great essential.* Let it be understood *and felt* that the column, announced to move at a given hour, will receive the command to forward march at the time specified, and not a moment later.

At the time fixed for forming battalions the trumpet sounds and the commanderies march to the battalion parade-grounds.

If commanderies are to move independently, still the oldest commandery is on the right, formed as prescribed; fifteen yards from its left is the right of the band of the next in rank, and so on.

GENERAL PARADE.

General Officers and their staffs should be mounted, or go on foot To ride in carriages is not military, nor is it exactly "the thing" for a chief in command. He takes position in front of the center of the line or on the flank of the column, but in a street parade should ride at the head of the column, so that the rear of his escort will be fifteen yards from the band of his leading commandery. The Adjutant General rides at his left and a little retired; the staff is in their rear formed in column of sections. A Standard Bearer should carry a banner, with the arms or name of the State thereon.

The instant his line is formed the Commanders of grand divisions should send a staff officer to the Commander in chief, to inform him of the fact.

A bugler should accompany each commander of grand divisions to sound the *attention, forward, halt,* etc., that all the battalions and commanderies may move together. The commander in chief should also be accompanied by a bugler, and his signals be promptly repeated by each Grand Division Commander's bugler.

Bands near together should never play at the same time, but take the time from the band in front.

The distance between Grand Divisions should be twenty yards.

A Battalion, too small to form a Grand Division, should join with others and form, according to seniority as one Grand Division.

A maneuver that would retard the rear of the column ought not to be permitted. If the leading commandery, by permission, executes any movement that causes it to lose ground, it should immediately take the double step to regain its distance. Each commandery either shortens or lengthens its steps, or executes some movement that will enable it to retain its proper place in the column; or commanderies execute maneuvers successively from the right of Grand Divisions. A signal from the commander in chief, repeated by Battalion Commanders, would enable maneuvers to be commenced simultaneously on the right of each Grand Division, and followed in succession by commanderies or simultaneously by every commandery in the column, according to previously promulgated orders

Gaps in the column, or the crowding together of grand or subdivisions should never be permitted, and each commanding officer ought to caution his subordinates and the guides on these points; complimenting them if they do well, and severely censuring any violation of this rule. Bands should also be instructed to take the full step and maintain their proper distance.

The carelessness of a single officer or Knight will destroy more of the harmony and beauty of the display than a whole Grand Division can neutralize; if, indeed, it can be overcome at all

To Pass in Review at General Parade.

If the column is to pass in review before the commander in chief the Battalion Commanders successively from the right, when they approach the station of the commander in chief, command:

1. *Pass in review.* 2. *Guide right.*

And the column continues the march, the bands do not wheel out of column, but if near together are careful to cease playing in time for the one in the rear to commence at fifteen yards from the station of the commander in chief

When a column passes in review it ought to be by commandery or division front, certainly not less than section front.

Bugle Signals.

These should be made a part of the instruction. The *assembly* is the signal for forming in ranks; if habitually sounded before forming the commandery it will be learned without effort.

The signals for drill are taught one or two at a time, until all are familiar with them.

A trumpet call embraces both the preparatory and executory commands, which are promptly repeated orally by the officers of subdivisions. Their frequent use will insure quick recognition, and the beauty of the signal drill will then be fully appreciated.

Movements to the right are on the ascending chord; corresponding movements to the left are corresponding signals on the descending chord; and changes of gait are all upon the same notes.

A person having "an ear for music" can easily learn to play upon the bugle or trumpet, and the principal signals can be learned in a surprisingly short space of time. It requires less study and practice than is necessary to commit the ritual to memory.

BUGLE SIGNALS. 209

1. ASSEMBLY OF MUSICIANS.

2. ASSEMBLY.

3. RECALL.

4. DRESS PARADE.

5. FLOURISH FOR REVIEW.

6. ATTENTION.

7. FORWARD.

8. HALT.

9. QUICK TIME.

BUGLE SIGNALS.

10. DOUBLE TIME

11. CHARGE.

12. GUIDE RIGHT.

13. GUIDE LEFT.

14. GUIDE CENTRE.

15. THREES RIGHT.

16. THREES LEFT.

17. THREES RIGHT ABOUT.

18. THREES LEFT ABOUT.

19. COLUMN RIGHT.

20. COLUMN LEFT.

21. RIGHT OBLIQUE.

22. LEFT OBLIQUE.

BUGLE SIGNALS. 213

23. RIGHT FRONT INTO LINE.
Moderate.

24. LEFT FRONT INTO LINE.
Moderate.

25. FACE TO THE REAR.
Slow.

26. ON RIGHT INTO LINE.
Moderate.

27. ON LEFT INTO LINE.
Moderate.

28. COMMANDERY RIGHT WHEEL.
Quick.

29. COMMANDERY LEFT WHEEL.

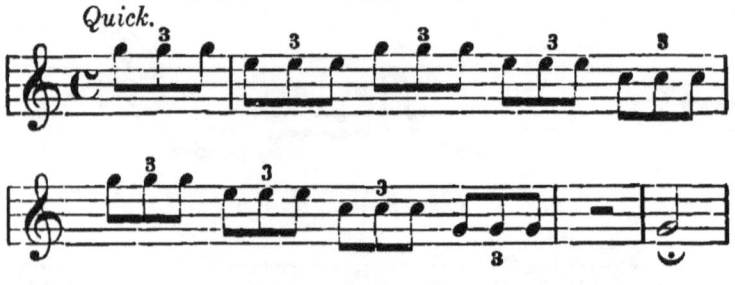

30. DEPLOY.

31. TO THE REAR.

32. BY THE RIGHT FLANK.

33. BY THE LEFT FLANK.

34. FUNERAL MARCH.

Very slow.

Repeat at will.

Award of Prize

AND RULES FOR COMPETITIVE DRILLS.

On occasions for the test of skill in military maneuvers there must be judges to "keep tally" and determine the relative merits of contestants.

The most skillful Board of Judges can not, with any degree of certainty, arrive at correct conclusions unless

1. They are familiar with the system of drill used.

2. Constantly near the commandery drilling; placing themselves on its flanks and in those proximate positions from which they can observe every movement to the best advantage.

3. They must score and record the degree of merit each separate movement is entitled to, and that before another movement is executed.

4. Each judge must have the same method of scoring and understand it before the drilling commences.

5. The commanderies should, as far as practicable, *execute the same movements in the same order*, and within the same limit of time.

The judges can *guess* as to the comparative merit of different commanderies, but they can not satisfactorily "score" them except upon the foregoing basis. To undertake to make up a score after the drilling is over is out of the question.

RULES FOR COMPETITIVE DRILLS.

It is better by far to prepare a schedule, and let the commanderies practice it than to undertake to judge of a " go as you please " drill.

When the aggregate score is made up, the chiefs of the several competing commanderies are notified of the time and place fixed for the public announcement and awarding of the prize, that each with his command may be present.

The following is recommended as a basis for

Rules for Competitive Drills.

1. Each commandery shall consist of eighteen* Knights and three as officers,† all of its own membership ‡

2. Each commandery shall drill separately, and in the order of rank,§ for forty minutes, unless the time be changed by unanimous consent of the officers in command of competing commanderies.

3 Three or five‖ disinterested experts shall be selected by the Committee on Drill as a Board of Judges, but they shall not be known as such to any others, until announced on the field ¶

4. The judges shall select their own method of scoring.

5. They shall have exclusive control of the field and commanderies during the drill.

---

*Not less than eighteen nor more than forty-eight. Fix the number definitely at 18, 24, 26, or 48

†One, Commander, or three, Commander and two Vice-Commanders, or six, Commander, Vice-Commander and Standard Guard.

‡It would be unjust to award a prize to a command permitted to pick or hire men from other commanderies or organizations for the occasion.

§The oldest has precedence and post of honor on every occasion; it would therefore be anything but fair to let it usurp the place belonging by right to a junior, or require the latter to hazard its rights by lot.

‖Five is better.   ¶Selected in time to become familiar with the system of drill to be used.

6. Except the judges, the commandery drilling, its band and standard guard, no person, whatever his rank or position may be, shall remain (even for a moment) on the field during or between drills.

7. Commanderies may drill with or without music, but the judges may require any movements to be executed without music, and the cadence shall be noted irrespective of the time kept by the band

8 The chiefs in charge of commanderies shall report at headquarters on the field thirty minutes before the contest is to commence; at which time they may determine by ballot whether the drill shall be witnessed by a contestant before his commandery has drilled. If not determined then, there shall be no such restriction.

9. Commanderies shall cease drilling at the second sound of the *recall* (made five minutes after its first sounding) at which the next commandery shall be ready, and at the *forward*, shall march on the field.

10. Want of promptness in responding to signals shall be treated as errors and marked against the delinquent.

11 * A schedule of movements shall be prepared by the judges. This may embrace any movement included in the "School of the Knight" "Manual of the Sword," (excluding the silent manual) "School of the Commandery," but none other.

12. Any movement passed will be marked "O," and can not be taken up afterward except by consent of judges.

13. Ten minutes may be allowed for display movements not embraced in the schedule, but these shall not be considered in any way in making up the score.

---

*This is not difficult for well-drilled commanderies, but if desired can be excepted. If the contest is likely to be close a schedule, though simple, is almost if not quite indispensable. Better let it be practiced any desired time before the drill than dispense with it.

Index.

Contents	3
Preface	5
Definitions	7

School of the Knight

Introduction	10
Commands (two kinds)	11
Position of body, limbs etc	11
To rest in place at parade	13, 15, 36
Attention	13, 37
Break ranks	13
Eyes right and left	13
Courtesy and discipline	14
Salutes; with hand, sword, banner in march	14, 30, 31, 43
Facings, right, left about	14, 15
Steps, length and cadence	15, 19
Step, balance	16
" short	17
" change	17, 18, 19
" side	18
" backward	18
" double	19
To march forward	16, 17
" halt	17
" mark time	17
" march backward	18
" " to rear	18
" " to side	18
To march in double time	19
" breathe	19
" dress by file	20
" dress right, left, back etc	20
The guide	21, 23
To march by flank	21
" " in column of files	21, 27
" change direction	22, 27
' oblique	23, 27

Wheelings

Wheel on fixed pivot	24
" on movable pivot	25
To turn	26
Double rank	26, 27

Sword Manual.

Remarks	28
"By the numbers."	29
To draw swords	29
" carry swords	30
" present	30, 31
" salute	31
" support	32, 34
" port swords	33
" order swords	33
" charge	34
" shoulder swords	34
" rear rest	35
" reverse	35
" rest sword arm	36
" parade rest	36
" resume attention	37

To open files	37, 38	To march threes to rear 62
" cross swords	38	" form line to left, etc. 63
" kneel and rise	39	" " " on right,
" return swords	39	etc 63, 64
" secure	40	" form line to front 65, 66
" inspect	41	" face " " rear 66, 67
" execute manual without command	42	" march line to rear 66 67
		" pass obstacle 67
" uncover (head)	41	" reform line 68
SCHOOL OF THE OFFICER.		The route step 68
General remarks and instruction	45	To form column of files 68
		" " threes from column of files 69
Past officers	49	
Positions in line (see different schools)		" form twos from line, and reverse 69
THE BAND AND DRUM MAJOR		" form single rank 70
General remarks and instruction	46	" " double rank 71, 72
		" close to double rank distance 72
SCHOOL OF THE COMMANDERY		
Remarks	49	" form divisions 72, 74
Past officers	49	" move or halt divisions 74, 75
Positions of officers, etc	50	
Subdivisions	50, 51	" oblique 75
Formations	51	" change directions 75 76
Counting off	52, 54	" face or march to rear 76
Position determined	54	" form line to left etc 77 78
To form in two ranks	55	
" dismiss commandery	55	" form line on left, etc 78
" open ranks	55, 56	" break into divisions 80
" close ranks	56	" re-form commandery 81
" march in line	56	" march by flank 82
" halt	56	" advance in threes to front 83
" wheel commandery	57	
" incline to right or left	58	" form line to front 84
" turn	58	" form column of threes from divisions and the reverse 84, 85
" march by flank	59	
" march threes to front	60	
" change direction	60, 61	THE DISPLAY DRILL
" halt and move forward	61	Remarks 86, 131
		To form column threes by flank 86
" oblique threes	61	

INDEX

To form line faced to
 rear . . . 87, 88
" form line by two
 movements . . . 88
" form line faced to rear
 by two movements 88
" to change front . . 89
" form line on standard 90
" form and wheel line 90
Column of sections from
 line 91
To wheel sections into
 line 91
Column of sections from
 threes 92
To form sections to right,
 etc 93
" break sections into
 threes 94
" form column threes
 from sections . 94
" form line from col.
 threes and sections
 by two movements 95
" form threes from sections and march to
 rear 95
" re form the sections 96
" form sections front to
 rear 97
" close sections to half
 distance . . . 97
" take wheeling (or
 other) distance . 98
" form sections forward
 from line . . . 98
" form line to front
 from sections . . 99
" form line by two
 movements from sections at half distance . . . 99 100
To form line by three
 movements 101, 102
" form twos from sections 103
" wheel for display . 103
" . " half of section 104
" advance sections in
 front of others . 105
" deploy column of
 sections . . 106-108
" form double sections 109
" break into sections
 from double section 110
" wheel subdivisions
 consecutively . 111
To change direction by
 flank of column of
 sections or double
 sections 113
" advance by flank of
 double sections . . 114
" break by flank to
 rear into column .
 . . . 114, 116
" deploy column .
 . . . . . 117, 121
" deploy in open order 121, 122
" close the column . 122
" " intervals only 123
" " to wheeling
 distance 123
" deploy line to
 front 123
" deploy line by
 flank 124
" extend intervals . 125
" close intervals . . 125
" march threes at
 open order by files

INDEX.

to rear 125
Order in echelon. . . 126
Movements in echelon.
 126-131
General remarks . . 131
FORMATION OF FIGURES.
To form Roman Cross
 from threes . . . 132
" form Greek Cross
 from threes . . . 134
" form Greek and
 Roman Crosses . 135
" display Greek Cross 136
" form Greek Cross
 from line 138
" form Greek Cross
 from square . . 156
" reduce Greek Cross
 by wheel to left . 154
" form Patriarchal
 Cross 140
" form Cross of Sa
 lem 142
" form St. Andrew's
 Cross 142
" form Triangle from
 files 145
" reduce Triangle . 146
" form triangle from
 column of threes .
 . . . . 147, 148
" form Triangle by
 threes 150
" form Triangle from
 sections . . . 150
" form Square from
 sections etc . . 152
" form Square from
 Greek Cross . . . 154
" form Star . . . 156
" form rays, circles,

etc., in " Star "
 formations . 156-159
SCHOOL OF THE BATTALION.
Remarks 160
New commands . . . 161
Officers 161
Officers' posts. . . . 164
Staff Officers 161
When to repeat com-
 mands 162
Rank of Commanderies 162
Equalizing Command-
 eries 163
The standards . . . 164
The markers 165
Formation of Battalion 166
To open ranks . 168, 170
" close ranks . . . 169
" dismiss battalion . 170
" march in line . . 170
" face and march to
 rear. 171
" oblique 172
" halt the batallion . 172
" rectify alignment .
 . . . . 173, 186
" give general al-
 ignment 173
" change direction of
 line 174
" march by the flank 175
" break into threes
 to march to left or
 right 176
" form line to the
 right or left . . . 176
Successive formation
 rules 177
To form line on right
 or left from column 178
" form line to front

INDEX

	from threes	178
To	form line to front faced to rear	179
"	form sections from line	181
"	form line from sections	181
"	form column of commanderies	182
"	form same and move forward	183
"	form same to rear from line	183
"	break from right, etc., to march to left	184
"	march column forward, halt, face, etc	184
"	change direction of column	185
"	put column in march and change direction	185
"	correct alignment	186
"	form line and move forward	187
"	form column to the flank	187
"	form line to front	185
"	form line to front faced to rear	189
"	form line by two movements	189
"	advance by flank of subdivisions	190
"	form line from subdivisions by flank	190
"	to form column by flank of subdivisions	191

To	march by flank of Subdivisions	191
"	form column of threes from column of commanderies, etc	191
"	close column to half section	192
"	form line to right or left from column at half distance	192
"	form Squadrons from Commanderies and the reverse	193
"	change front	194

CEREMONIES.

Dress Parade 195
Review 200
General Parade . . 204

BUGLE SIGNALS . . 208

1 Assembly of Musicians 209
2 Assembly 209
3 Recall 209
4 Dress Parade . . . 210
5 Flourish for Review 210
6 Attention 210
7 Forward 210
8 Halt 210
9 Quick Time . . . 210
10 Double Time . . . 211
11 Charge 211
12 Guide right . . . 211
13 Guide left 211
14 Guide center . . . 211
15 Threes right . . . 211
16 Threes left . . . 212
17 Threes right about . 212
18 Threes left about . 212
19 Column right . . 212

20 Column left . . . 212
21 Right oblique . . 212
22 Left oblique . . . 212
23 Right front into line 213
24 Left front into line . 213
25 Face to the rear . . 213
26 On right into line . 213
27 On left into line . . 213
28 Commandery right wheel 213
29 Commandery left wheel 214
30 Deploy 214
31 To the rear . . . 214
32 By the right flank . 214
33 By the left flank . 214
34 Funeral March . . 215
Award of Prizes and Rules for Competitive Drills 216

www.ingramcontent.com/pod-product-compliance
Lightning Source LLC
Chambersburg PA
CBHW021845230426
43669CB00008B/1089